A
Hobbit
Devotional

Ed Strauss

SHILOH RUN  PRESS
An Imprint of Barbour Publishing, Inc.

Print ISBN 978-1-63058-490-0

eBook Editions:
Adobe Digital Edition (.epub) 978-1-63058-977-6
Kindle and MobiPocket Edition (.prc) 978-1-63058-978-3

Original Cover design by Kirk DouPonce, DogEared Design

Published by Shiloh Run Press, an imprint of Barbour Publishing, Inc., P.O. Box 719, Uhrichsville, Ohio 44683 www.barbourbooks.com

Our mission is to publish and distribute inspirational products offering exceptional value and biblical encouragement to the masses.

Member of the
Evangelical Christian
Publishers Association

Printed in China.

Contents

Introduction: The Heart of *The Hobbit* 7

1. Out of Our Comfort Zones 11

2. A Welcome Rabble-Rouser 17

3. Uninvited Guests 21

4. A Reversal of Fortunes 27

5. Solid and Adventurous 33

6. A Not-So-Funny Phobia 37

7. Little People, Great Deeds 41

8. Hearts Set on Pilgrimage 47

9. When God Isn't There 51

10. Pride Goes Before a Fall 55

11. Watch and Pray 59

12. God Is in the Details 63

13. The Sword of the Spirit 67

14. The Road to Rivendell 73

15. Taking Counsel with the Wise 79

16. Someone Has to Do It 83

17. Checking Things Out 87

18. The Goblins' Return 93

19. Of Wizards and Magic 99

20. Looking for a Way Out 105

21. Compassion for the Fallen 109

22. The Rings of Power 115

23. A Nearly Derailed Miracle 121

24. Counting Your Blessings 127

25. Being a Decent Fellow 131

26. Stepping into Your Dream. 135

27. Snatched Away by Eagles 139

28. A Fierce and Flawed Friend. 145

29. Waiting till It's Time 149

30. Forgetting the Forest 153

31. Overcoming a Deep Fear. 157

32. The Dark Night of the Soul. 161

33. Adrenaline and Love 165

34. The Saruman Conspiracy. 169

35. Adventure on Indefinite Hold 175

36. Good Luck or Blessing 179

37. Not What We Expected 185

38. The Fortunate Misfortune 189

39. Pleasant Legends, Potent Prophecies. 195

40. Doubting the Dragon 199

41. When False Hope Dies 205

42. Waiting for an Open Door 211

43. Called Upon Yet Again 217

44. Facing the Dragon. 221

45. It Comes with the Territory. 225

46. Reaching Your Potential 229

47. The Effect of Dragon Talk. 235

48. A Noble Friend 241

49. A Kingly Gift 245

50. Bard the Grim Bowman 251

51. Messengers Bearing Messages. 257

52. Thranduil's Disaster Relief. 263

53. Catching the Dragon Sickness 269
54. A Misunderstood Friend 275
55. Tearing Down Walls 281
56. A Time for Wild Bears 287
57. Simple Pleasures and Priorities 291
58. Faraway, Enchanting Lands 295
59. A Heavenly Haven 299
60. Your Place in God's Plans 303
Glossary of Terms 307
Timeline of *The Hobbit* 312
Sources 316
Notes 317

Introduction:
The Heart of The Hobbit

J.R.R. Tolkien wrote *The Hobbit* as a children's story, and its bumbling, lighthearted humor mingled with frightful images and grim realism made it an instant classic when it appeared in 1937. When his publisher urged him to write a sequel, Tolkien set out to do just that, writing the first chapter that same year. But what slowly emerged from the deep wells of his imagination was not another children's tale, but a mature story with a complex plot structure. Written in epic style, set against the sweeping panorama of Middle-earth, Tolkien created *The Lord of the Rings*.

 The Hobbit is most definitely the prequel to *The Lord of the Rings*. In fact, in the latter Frodo picks up the adventure precisely where his uncle Bilbo left off in *The Hobbit*.

Yet the stylistic divide—and the difference in attention to details—is so pronounced that if you try to compare the two books you might be told, "Remember, *The Hobbit* is a children's story!" For some, a simpler book can't be taken as seriously as *The Lord of the Rings*.

This is, I believe, a mistake. Despite its differences in style, *The Hobbit* contains just as many serious scenes; the dangers it describes are just as real; and the struggles its characters endure are just as pronounced. And although *The Hobbit* starts off humorously, deeper and darker themes begin to emerge quickly, almost completely dominating the story. Tolkien noted that "the tone and style change with the Hobbit's development, passing from fairy-tale to the noble and high."[1] In addition, profound emotions such as fear, insecurity, loneliness, hopelessness, and despair are prevalent—relentlessly so—throughout the story, which finally culminates in a terrific clash of armies as desperate as the Battle of the Pelennor Fields.

Nevertheless, many people who read *The Lord of the Rings* (or see the movies) before reading *The Hobbit* are surprised by its more whimsical tone and characterizations. Tolkien was aware of this issue and in 1960 began to rewrite *The Hobbit* as a more formal, epic novel. After writing the first three chapters, however, he abandoned the project, realizing that much of the rapid pacing and charm of his original story was being lost. He therefore decided on only a few revisions, leaving the story mainly as he had written it.

In *The Hobbit* Tolkien repeatedly shows Bilbo and the dwarves overcoming fear with courage, discouragement with tenacity, and despair with hope. Because we today also face constant challenges—in our finances, our careers, and our personal lives—we can draw encouragement from this story. I therefore invite you to take a long, deep look with me into the heart of *The Hobbit*.

ED STRAUSS
AUGUST 2011

1

Out of Our Comfort Zones

In a hole in the ground there lived a hobbit. . . .
It was a hobbit hole, and that means comfort.
THE HOBBIT, CHAPTER I

A very long time ago—so J.R.R. Tolkien tells us—a small, happy people called hobbits lived in a comfortable corner of Middle-earth known as the Shire.

Bilbo Baggins was one of the most comfort-loving hobbits of all. He came from a respectable, well-to-do family and enjoyed the luxury of a hobbit hole inside a hill featuring several bedrooms, washrooms, kitchens, dining rooms, and wardrobes. Like all hobbits, Bilbo Baggins ate six meals a day when he could get them—and he usually could.

Now, most hobbits didn't experience quite as much luxury as Bilbo, but they still filled their dwellings with as many comforts and conveniences as they could. Hobbits worked hard to get such things, but they were accustomed to plenty in their pleasant, good land.

Like the hobbits, we in the modern West are quite prosperous compared with most others in the world. We have to work hard for our good things, true—but our work is generally rewarded: Our homes are comfortable and modern, and we eat good food, wear fashionable clothes, and enjoy quite a few luxuries beyond our actual needs.

It's great to live in a land of peace and plenty. And there's nothing wrong with enjoying our comforts and conveniences like big-screen TVs and all the latest gadgets. But being surrounded by material things can *create* a problem for us. It did for the hobbits.

As Tolkien tells us, the hobbits became so comfortable and self-absorbed that they paid less and less attention to what was happening in the lands around them "until they came to think that peace and plenty were the rule in Middle-earth."[2]

Of course, that *wasn't* how things were. Much of Middle-earth was falling into desperate times. A dark lord named Sauron (under the guise of the Necromancer) was entrenched in his stronghold in Mirkwood and beginning to mobilize armies of orcs. In the ancient land of Eriador, trolls were descending from their mountain haunts and devouring whole villages. East of the Misty Mountains, goblins and wargs were plotting to wipe out entire settlements of men. Goblin armies were brooding in Gundabad and would soon attempt to overrun the North. And there was Smaug the dragon.

But the hobbits, comfortably sheltered in the Shire, neither knew nor cared about the rest of the world.

Over four thousand years ago, some Israelites had a similar blind spot. The Canaanite warlord of Hazor had conquered the northern half of their country and oppressed them for twenty years. Then a soldier named Barak—urged by the judge Deborah—called the Israelites to rise up and fight. Tribes like Zebulun and Naphtali rushed into combat and fought heroically, risking their lives in the deadliest parts of the battlefield, but tribes like Reuben and Dan and Asher didn't even show. They sat around campfires watching their flocks or remained on the seacoast, loading their ships. Apparently, the Canaanites weren't *their* problem. They had peace and plenty and little concern over problems in the rest of their country (see Judges 4:1–7; 5:15–18).

But they *should* have been concerned—just as we should be moved by others' problems as well.

Some days it's perfectly fine to eat a second breakfast, curl up on the couch, and enjoy a TV show. But that can't be our whole life. At times we need to step *out* of our comfort zones and show concern for the world beyond our living room. No one person can solve all the planet's problems, of course—but an important first step is to be aware of those distant (and not-so-distant) places full of dark things like famines and wars and poverty. Many people desperately need a helping hand.

When we hear of floods or earthquakes, we can, of course, donate money. But stepping outside our comfort zone means more than just giving cash—it might mean rolling up our sleeves and getting involved personally, at a local charity or community organization or our church. And don't overlook helping your own family members in need.

Any worthy cause that improves even a small part of the world is worth giving ourselves to. We don't have to march to Lonely Mountain and back since there are needs right in our own communities, desperate situations right outside our doors.

When God blesses us with peace and plenty and leisure, that gives us an opportunity. Rather than hoarding our things and spending time on ourselves, we should enjoy what we have *and* reach out to others. Whether or not we have two chests full of treasure—like Bilbo at the end of his adventure—we'll do well to help the needy around us.

> *Don't look out only for your own interests,*
> *but take an interest in others, too.*
> PHILIPPIANS 2:4 NLT

2

A Welcome Rabble-Rouser

"I mean, you used to upset things badly in these
parts once upon a time. I beg your pardon,
but I had no idea you were still in business."
THE HOBBIT, CHAPTER 1

When Gandalf identified himself to Bilbo, the hobbit immediately remembered parties where the wizard told spellbinding tales of dragons and goblins and giants. Bilbo recalled—and raved over—Gandalf's spectacular fireworks displays. Then he stopped and asked warily if this was by chance *the* same Gandalf who, in years past, had talked impressionable young hobbits into "going off into the Blue for mad adventures."[3]

Yes indeed—the same Gandalf. (As if there were others of that name running around.)

Bilbo's coming adventure was by no means the first that Gandalf had arranged in the Shire. The wizard had a reputation for getting quiet, respectable hobbits to do strange things—such as running away to see elves or sailing off in ships to distant lands. Shire-folk even considered climbing trees risky business!

To be sure, hobbits enjoyed hearing Gandalf's tales, but most of them didn't want to have an adventure of their own. So when Gandalf said he was looking for someone to share in a quest, Bilbo quickly replied that the wizard was searching the wrong neighborhood. Hobbits *here* were settled, common-sense folk who didn't like unusual things to disrupt their daily schedule—thank you very much.

Thrill-seekers among us might want to write off Bilbo as a stick in the mud. *Boring!* Where's his sense of adventure?

But the hobbit had a point: while adventures *do* inject excitement into our lives, they are not entirely a rush of fun on a roller coaster. Being part of a great adventure is more than just enjoying new experiences; it can also be sticking to a dull, difficult path when our mind and body scream to run off to the right or left. Great adventures often involve tough choices and lonely stands for what we know to be true. They may require forging on when it would be so much easier to turn back.

And adventures often come along at inconvenient times. They can seem more like interruptions than exciting opportunities. Like Bilbo, few of us really welcome rabble-rousers who appear on our doorstep with *those* kinds of adventures—the ones that throw our carefully planned schedules (and lives) into an uproar.

Unless. . .the adventure is for a very great cause, and brings very great rewards.

Following Jesus offers great rewards, and that's why He delights in stirring us up—in sending us off into the Blue on mad adventures. Just as Gandalf was fully aware of how some people viewed him ("They say I am a nuisance and a disturber of the peace"[4]), Jesus heard the same kinds of things from His opponents: "He stirs up the people all over Judea by his teaching" (Luke 23:5 NIV). And indeed He did. Today, Jesus rouses *us* to action, and for those who love Him, He's a most welcome rabble-rouser.

For two thousand years Jesus has called people to discipleship—the greatest adventure of all. In every generation, Christians have put their faith in Jesus and followed Him into exciting (and sometimes very difficult) adventures. We might wonder, "But is the adventure of discipleship for *today*?" Yes, definitely. Jesus hasn't changed, since He is "the same yesterday, today, and forever" (Hebrews 13:8 NKJV).

Jesus still says, "Come, follow me." And He says, "Whoever wants to be my disciple must deny themselves" (Matthew 4:19; 16:24 NIV). That may mean giving up things we enjoy, the daily comforts we've become used to. Some may follow Mother Teresa's footsteps to the slums of Calcutta, but for most of us, following Jesus happens in Hometown, U.S.A. There, we'll live sacrificially, looking for opportunities to serve, being open to Jesus' adventure every day.

There will be excitement—sometimes more than we wish for—and there will be hardships. We'll probably experience dreary times when it seems like we're trudging through darkness with no end in sight. Fortunately, there will probably *not* be giant spiders to battle.

But for all the trouble and discomfort we'll face, Jesus has promised great rewards—and not only in heaven. There's a great satisfaction here and now that comes from knowing we're giving our lives to a good and noble cause.

Like Gandalf, Jesus is more than just a great storyteller—He calls people to follow Him in a self-sacrificing way. Like Gandalf, Jesus is "still in the business" of arranging grand adventures. If you'll follow Him through hardships and persecution, He promises that "your reward is great in heaven" (Luke 6:23 NKJV).

3

Uninvited Guests

*He liked visitors, but he liked to know them before
they arrived, and he preferred to ask them himself.*
THE HOBBIT, CHAPTER I

Bilbo certainly did like visitors. His hallway had "lots
and lots of pegs for hats and coats,"[5] indicating he
didn't expect one or two guests at a time. He liked his
house *full*.

Now, all hobbits were hospitable, but Bilbo took feasting and merry-making to a new level. He was a regular
party animal. Remember the party he threw on his hundred and eleventh birthday—*the* party? (See the first chapter of *The Fellowship of the Ring*.) The Shire had never seen

such an extravagant celebration.

And *the party* wasn't an isolated incident. Tolkien doesn't describe every bash Bilbo hosted, but we can be quite sure that he had them. There he was, a well-to-do bachelor, living alone in a huge hobbit hole with many bedrooms for guests. Bilbo had enough beds to accommodate thirteen dwarves at once, though a few had to sleep on couches.

Mr. Baggins loved playing host; he just wanted to know who his guests were and when they were coming. He was not so fond of strangers showing up unannounced. So when those thirteen dwarves knocked on his door, trooped in, and made themselves at home, Bilbo was rather put out. After hurrying to his kitchen to load food and drink on trays, he became very hot, red in the face, and annoyed.

The hobbit didn't *know* these dwarves—he hadn't invited them, yet they had barged in and imposed on his kindness, ordering raspberry jam and mince-pies, cheese and salad, tea and coffee, eggs, cold chicken, pickles, and cakes as if he were a waiter. Bilbo was flustered. Worse, he had a growing fear that he might run out of pastries and other food. Not only would that embarrass him, but Shire custom dictated a host feed his guests first—even if the host himself had to go hungry!

Mr. Baggins didn't enjoy last-minute scrambles. He didn't like food to run out. His one hundred and eleventh birthday party was an example of the way he preferred to do things. Presents were ordered a *year* ahead of time. Wagons of party supplies arrived *weeks* early. Food deliveries were organized and punctual. Invitations were sent out to select guests, and Bilbo meticulously ticked off names as he received replies accepting his invitations.

The unexpected party, on the other hand, was *not* Bilbo's type, and dwarves were *not* his kind of guests. Early on, Bilbo had even wished that *Gandalf* would leave. The wizard was bad enough. But dwarves? They took the cake—literally.

The unexpected party was no fun at all, and parties are supposed to be fun, aren't they? Doesn't common sense dictate that parties are *happy* times?

Yes, they are—and God loves a good party, too. He commanded the Israelites to celebrate several joyful feasts during the year, and in the parable of the prodigal son, Jesus compared God to a father who shouted, "Let's have a feast and celebrate" (Luke 15:23 NIV). Soon there was food and music and dancing.

God wants us to enjoy celebrations with our friends and family. He wants us to enjoy good times and good food with our loved ones. But there's more to the story than that. He also calls us to be cheerful hosts at inconvenient times—and He expects us to be welcoming even when the guests aren't the kind of people we'd normally invite.

Out of fairness to Bilbo, most of *us* don't like it when strange people show up unannounced and we're ransacking the fridge and cupboards trying to find food for them. Most of us wouldn't have been half as hospitable as Bilbo if thirteen hungry, bearded strangers showed up at our doorstep. Yet the apostle Peter tells us, "Be hospitable to one another without grumbling" (1 Peter 4:9 NKJV).

Jesus went a step further when He said, "When you give a luncheon or dinner, do not invite your friends, your brothers or sisters, your relatives, or your rich neighbors; if you do, they may invite you back and so you will be repaid. But when you give a banquet, invite the poor, the crippled, the lame, the blind, and you will be blessed" (Luke 14:12–14 NIV). The book of Hebrews adds: "Don't forget to show hospitality to strangers, for some who have done this have entertained angels without realizing it!" (Hebrews 13:2 NLT).

It seems that hungry dwarves are just the kind of folks who'd appear on Jesus' banquet list.

Most of the uninvited guests at our doors will be neither angels nor dwarves. But they might be odd characters, not part of the "popular crowd." They might be relatives we're not completely delighted to see. In those moments, it may be difficult to follow Jesus' words. But the Bible is clear: If we want to be blessed, we need to be cheerful and hospitable.

4

A Reversal of Fortunes

"After that we went away, and we have had to
earn our livings as best we could. . .sinking as
low as blacksmith-work or even coalmining."
THE HOBBIT, CHAPTER 1

Dwarves had a reputation for being materialistic, greedy for gold and jewels. But they were very hard workers, so when they managed to strike a mother lode and become rich, well. . .they'd earned it.

Skilled artisans, dwarves not only carved awe-inspiring palaces in stone, they created jewelry of breathtaking beauty. So it was with Thorin's people: His great-grandfather had found the Arkenstone, a gem unlike any other, and his grandfather Thror had hoarded vast quantities of gold and jewels under Lonely Mountain. They established the kingdom of Erebor and were fabulously prosperous and happy.

Then the dragon came, bringing death, misery, and poverty.

In one terrible night of burning and horror, catastrophe overwhelmed the dwarves. Many were slain, and those who survived fled. While the foul worm inhabited their great halls and slept upon their wealth, the dwarves went south "into long and homeless wandering."[6] They wandered up and down the land, taking whatever work they could find, mining coal and blacksmithing. Afterward, they settled in the Blue Mountains, northwest of the Shire. They earned a living, but it was pitiful compared to what they'd lost. Thorin became king, heir to the House of Durin, but spent his entire adult life as a common laborer.

Maybe *dwarvish greed* is a strong phrase in Thorin's context. Should we have a little empathy instead?

Another long-ago people suffered a similar loss—and warrant a similar sympathy.

In 586 BC the Jewish people's land of Judah was attacked by the Babylonian king Nebuchadnezzar—whom some versions of the Bible describe as a great dragon. Jerusalem and the temple were set ablaze, and all their gold and treasures taken. The Jews themselves were marched away as impoverished exiles to the land of Babylon. Jeremiah described these events metaphorically, saying, "King Nebuchadnezzar of Babylon has eaten and crushed us and drained us of strength. He has swallowed us like a great monster and filled his belly with our riches. He has thrown us out of our own country" (Jeremiah 51:34 NLT). The King James Version uses more vivid imagery, saying that Nebuchadnezzar "swallowed me up like a dragon."

Those were deep, deep losses—which many of us have experienced as well. Or perhaps we've seen family and friends suffer such financial setbacks, and we understand the pain and hardship that accompany these tragedies. Our sympathy for the fabulously rich who lose their fortunes through bad judgment is probably small—but we can certainly empathize when a loved one loses a once-secure job and their home as a result.

Some people try to put a positive spin on hard times by saying, "It's only money." But a lack of "only money" can cast a long shadow on people's lives, requiring them to make difficult choices—like working multiple part-time jobs for low wages. The psychological blow of seeing years of hard work wiped out can be overwhelming.

So we empathize. The Bible tells us to "weep with those who weep" (Romans 12:15 NKJV).

We don't have to lose vast wealth or a lavish home to

identify with these feelings. Tragedy strikes in many ways, affecting all levels of society. A workplace accident may cause years of pain and hardship. Chronic illness forces some to curtail much of their previous way of life.

In this context, perhaps we'll begin to understand Thorin's profound sense of loss, his longing for justice, his desire for his kingdom to be restored, and—yes—even his hope of regaining his fortune. As Gandalf observed, if Thorin could retake even a small part of his ancestral wealth or reclaim a family heirloom, that would have served as a balm for his pain.[7]

For the Jewish people, God restored their fortunes after they'd languished in Babylon for seventy years. He had promised, "I will punish Bel, the god of Babylon, and make him vomit up all he has eaten" (Jeremiah 51:44 NLT). And the Babylonian dragon did bring up his stolen loot, just as God predicted. When the Persians conquered Babylon, they gave the temple gold back to the Jews and allowed them to return to their land (see Ezra 1).

When the dragon of tragedy swallows a valuable part of our lives, we can hope and pray that God's promise to the Israelites will work for us as well. Sometimes we'll enjoy God's wonderful restoration, while other times we'll have to accept our situation and adjust to a new normal. We can't, on our own, command a dragon to cough up our old fortunes.

But God blessed the Jews—at least they regained their precious gold. If it's God's will, He'll do it for *you*, too. He may at least restore a portion of your treasure.

5

Solid and Adventurous

Then something Tookish woke up inside him, and he
wished to go and see the great mountains, and hear the
pine-trees and the waterfalls, and explore the caves.
THE HOBBIT, CHAPTER I

Bilbo lived in Hobbiton, where many years earlier his father, Bungo Baggins, had married the celebrated Belladonna Took. Now, the Tooks were a large clan of hobbits to the south in Green Hill country. (Took rhymes with *kook*, by the way.) The Bagginses were considerably more practical, predictable, and respectable than the Green Hill folk—after all, several Tooks had gone off on wild adventures. Nevertheless, the risk-taking Tooks were even wealthier than the Bagginses. Go figure.

The Tooks were natural leaders among hobbits. Tooks were "somewhat bolder and more adventurous" than the average Shire-folk.[8] They were known for their daring deeds and boasted of producing some of the greatest heroes. In fact, the hereditary title Thain (leader of the Shire) was passed down to the head of the Took family.

In the beginning of this story, the Baggins side of Bilbo's nature dominated, almost smothering his Tookish side. Many of us are Baggins-minded as well. We're down-to-earth and rational. Oh, to be sure, we have our dreams—and every once in a while we stoke their glowing coals in our imagination. But we're either too "sensible" to follow the dream, or hard experience has sent us, chastised, back to the safe confines of a daily routine. We fulfill our desire for adventure by riding a motorcycle on the weekends or renting an action movie on a Friday night.

And so our larger dreams go unfulfilled.

That's what had happened to Bilbo. His idealism had, over the years, been displaced by a more practical nature. Deep down, Bilbo still longed to see the wide world, to venture beyond the tame edges of his homeland—but he had settled down. He now fulfilled his youthful longings by taking extended walks around the Shire. Marking his favorite paths in red ink on his wall map, Bilbo took those same walks again and again. The dream had been replaced by a comfortable and quite manageable daydream.

Then a stirring dwarf song—and dwarves can *sing*!—awakened Bilbo's desire to venture out, even if that meant abandoning the safe world he knew.

For most of us—hobbit or modern humans—it's easier to be adventuresome when we're "young and foolish." Adventure is practically built into our young bodies. But, as we age, we desire more security. This is particularly true if we marry and have children. Suddenly our carefree, risk-taking lifestyle seems out of place. Backpacking through Europe is no longer a viable option, so we get a "solid job." We settle down into predictable schedules. And that's all fine and necessary. . .as long as we don't sink into immobility and completely lose our edge.

It's great to enjoy an action movie on Friday night—and if you get a thrill from roaring down the highway on a motorbike, go for it. But these "adventures" fall well within our comfort zones. We're more likely to avoid those chaotic experiences, where things happen unexpectedly and events are beyond our control. Those things that disrupt our stable plans or derail our set schedules are not quite welcome.

When Gandalf searched his memory for the ideal hobbit to join dwarves on a long adventure, he realized he wanted someone with a good, practical head on his shoulders. Someone solid and unflinching—such as a Baggins. The tough road ahead would require a stalwart soul who'd stay the course after the novelty wore off and the tedium set in. The ideal candidate also needed a little Took blood to get him started on the adventure in the first place—just not so much that he was an erratic, flighty "fool of a Took."[9]

Bilbo fit the bill perfectly.

Like Bilbo, we have a deep and genuine need for security. But we can't do without change, or we'll simply stagnate. If we never expand our horizons, we'll settle into deep mental ruts—maybe permanently. We need both security *and* a sense of adventure.

Jesus warned that those who followed Him needed to be committed. "No one," He said, "having put his hand to the plow, and looking back, is fit for the kingdom of God" (Luke 9:62 NKJV). He also cautioned regarding "those who hear the message and immediately receive it with joy. But since they don't have deep roots, they don't last long. They fall away as soon as they have problems or are persecuted for believing God's word" (Mark 4:16–17 NLT).

Let's plan to last. Let's be committed to persevering in our Christian walk—in fact, to any venture to which we're called.

Are you a Baggins or a Took—or, like Bilbo, a blend of the two?

6

A Not-So-Funny Phobia

Then he fell flat on the floor, and kept on calling out "struck by lightning, struck by lightning!" over and over again.
THE HOBBIT, CHAPTER 1

Just after the dwarves' song had awakened a wanderlust in Bilbo, he glanced out his window and saw someone lighting a fire in the distance—and it made him think of marauding dragons setting his pleasant hill ablaze. The thought frightened him so badly that he tried to leave the room and hide in his cellar until the visiting dwarves went away. They caught him trying to slip off, however. So much for *that* idea.

Mere moments later (talk about bad timing!) Thorin,

sitting in almost total darkness, stated grimly that some of the group might not survive their adventure. At that point Bilbo had a panic attack, falling to his knees and shaking like a jelly—a dessert with which he was quite familiar. Some primal fear seized Bilbo, and an uncontainable shriek rose up inside, building in intensity. When it erupted, the dwarves sprang to their feet, knocking over the table. Gandalf lit a magical light on the end of his staff, and Bilbo fell prostrate on the floor, repeating hysterically, "Struck by lightning! Struck by lightning!"

It sounds outlandishly funny. But it wasn't really.

Tolkien doesn't explain what spurred this outburst, but it's unlikely that Mr. Baggins had ever been struck by lightning. More probably, he knew someone who had suffered such a fate—or he'd been traumatized by a lightning storm as a child. Whatever the case, all this talk of dragon-fire and dying had rekindled a deep-seated dread in Bilbo. The fear was very real in him, however irrational it seemed to others. Fear of lightning even has a name: *astraphobia*.

Had Bilbo not mastered that fear, it would certainly have held him back from his great adventure.

At times, potent anxiety keeps us from attempting great things. Deep-buried fears, however laughable they seem in the light of day, can paralyze us—unless we overcome them by an effort of will. And that's what Bilbo did.

Determined to prove that he was not good for nothing, Bilbo steeled his resolve and boldly told the dwarves that they had to but name the task and he'd attempt it. Yes, he'd become soft over the years, but Gandalf was quite right when he said that hobbits were capable of great acts of courage in a crisis. They could rise to the occasion. This was such a moment.

And wouldn't you know it, two months later, in a high mountain pass, he was caught in a terrific lightning storm, an astraphobic's worst nightmare. But Bilbo was not, contrary to his fears, sizzled by lightning.

In the Bible, God told a man named Gideon to lead the Israelites against an army of invaders called the Midianites. The angel of the Lord called Gideon a "mighty warrior," yet this "hero" had to overcome a great deal of fear and doubt to even *begin* to do what God told him. Gideon protested, "My clan is the weakest in the whole tribe of Manasseh, and I am the least in my entire family!" (Judges 6:15 NLT). Fear had such a grip on Gideon that again and again he asked God for signs to assure him that he was capable.

The night before the battle, as he sat in the hills above the Midianite camp, Gideon was still afraid. God finally told him, "If you are afraid to attack, go down to the camp . . .and listen to what they are saying. Afterward, you will be encouraged to attack the camp" (Judges 7:10–11 NIV). Gideon was indeed encouraged and went on to win a tremendous victory.

What was the secret of his success?

In spite of the fear and doubt that fought to hold him back, Gideon was (eventually) willing to look beyond them and believe God. He made a deliberate effort of his will to conquer those fears and to trust the Lord.

An old axiom says that courage is not the absence of fear but the willingness to proceed in spite of it. As we step out to follow the Lord, faith and courage take root in our hearts and displace the fear. God tells us, "Fear not, for I am with you; be not dismayed, for I am your God. I will strengthen you, yes, I will help you" (Isaiah 41:10 NKJV). And He will.

Gideon's quest was to drive out the Midianite invaders who robbed and pillaged Israel. Bilbo's quest was to take back the gold and treasure a dragon had stolen from the dwarves.

What is your quest? What fears hold you back from launching out? Are you willing to believe God and overcome those fears?

7

Little People, Great Deeds

*"I have chosen Mr. Baggins and that ought to be enough
for all of you. . . . There is a lot more in him than you guess,
and a deal more than he has any idea of himself."*
THE HOBBIT, CHAPTER 1

From the beginning, Thorin had had his doubts about
Bilbo. In fact, the dwarf leader was opposed to bringing *any* hobbit on the quest from the moment Gandalf
had mentioned the idea.

Dwarves had low opinions of Shire-folk. To and from
their home in the Blue Hills, Thorin's people often walked
the east-west road through the Shire—and as far as they
could see, hobbits were nothing more than simple farmers,

mere food producers. Bilbo was, in their opinion, more likely to be a grocer than a treasure hunter.

And there was some truth in that attitude. Bilbo certainly did like his food. He kept a well-stocked larder. But as Thorin and the proud dwarves were to learn, there was much more to hobbits than their ability to eat. And there was a great deal more to Bilbo himself.

Some time would pass, however, before that became clear to Thorin.

He'd originally had a high opinion of Gandalf's wisdom—so much so that Thorin had sought the wizard's advice on how to conquer the dragon and retake his treasure. Though his kingdom had been shattered—though his people were reduced in number and living in exile—Thorin was thinking of traditional ways of forging alliances and sending soldiers to confront Smaug. But Gandalf told Thorin the only solution was to use *stealth*—to enlist the services of a quiet-footed hobbit.

Thorin was frustrated. He couldn't see the sense in that and began to believe that Gandalf was simply entangling him with the Shire-folk as some kind of joke. But Gandalf dearly loved hobbits—and after long years of dealing with them, he had perceived that beneath their jovial appearance was an unusual strength. And yes, they were capable of moving exceptionally quietly.

So when Thorin made disparaging remarks about hobbits, Gandalf decided to send one on the quest to *prove* that great things can be accomplished by the despised and insignificant.[10]

The same principle applies in our lives. As the apostle Paul wrote, "God has chosen the foolish things of the world to put to shame the wise, and God has chosen the weak things of the world to put to shame the things which are mighty. . .and the things which are despised God has chosen" (1 Corinthians 1:27–28 NKJV).

Sure, God *could* choose the strong and the wise to accomplish his purposes. Sometimes He does. But then we and they might think the strong and wise succeeded because they *were* strong or wise. We wouldn't see God at work.

And we'd never discover the hidden strength that God has placed inside each of us who don't seem to be particularly strong. . .or smart. . .or talented. We wouldn't learn how God can cause us to be "strengthened with might through His Spirit in the inner man" (Ephesians 3:16 NKJV).

Each of us has godly potential—more than we'll ever know. The Bible describes us as ordinary-looking clay pots but goes on to say that God has hidden great treasure within us (2 Corinthians 4:7). So don't let outward appearances deceive you. Don't be quick to judge others based on superficial appearances. And don't be too quick to limit *yourself.*

Maybe you can't do a job in your own strength. But with God's help? That's an entirely different matter! God shows that He is God when He does great things using weak, despised means—since we obviously *can't* do such things on our own.

When the weak accomplish mighty things, it shames the strong who rely on their own power, who tend to leave God out of the equation. They're confounded when they see towering Goliaths fall before much weaker Davids. They realize there has to be something *more* at work—some greater power.

That, of course, is the point God is making.

For the dwarves assembled in Bilbo's parlor, such realization was still future. They simply had Gandalf's word that taking a hobbit—*this* hobbit—on their quest was a good idea.

The dwarves' knowledge of Gandalf was limited, but his reputation had spread throughout the land of Eriador— so they'd heard that he was a wise and powerful wizard. Gandalf told the dwarves that *he* had chosen Bilbo and that ought to be enough for them. His unspoken message: "Trust me on this one."

Today, God asks us to trust Him in the same way. He

often chooses to use weak, despised people—including us—if we can only trust that He knows what He's doing. When He chooses imperfect means to accomplish His perfect purposes, let's recall that *He* indeed has done the choosing—and that ought to be enough for us.

8

Hearts Set on Pilgrimage

"I wish I was at home in my nice hole by the fire,
with the kettle just beginning to sing!" It was
not the last time that he wished that!
THE HOBBIT, CHAPTER 2

When Mr. Baggins awoke the next morning, the dwarves had already devoured breakfast and left the house. Bilbo was certainly happy about that! Thank goodness they'd set off without him and that his life could now get back to normal. (After cleaning up the monstrous mess they'd left in his kitchen, that is.)

Then Gandalf popped in and pointed out Thorin's note, telling Bilbo to meet the dwarves at the Green Dragon Inn.

The hobbit was so flustered that when the wizard urged him to leave immediately, he did precisely that. He took off running down the road and arrived just as the dwarves were about to set out.

Now, when Thorin and company began their journey, they first passed east through the Shire—land the hobbit knew well. Later they rode through lonesome lands, where the roads grew steadily worse, and passed ruins of ancient, abandoned castles. It was May and sunshiny, but as June approached, the rains began. Soon Bilbo, Gandalf, and the dwarves were wet and cold. After a day of unrelenting rain soaking his clothes and leaking into the food packs, Bilbo began to realize that "adventures are not all pony-rides in May-sunshine."[11]

He got that right. Quests inevitably involve hardships and privations.

And this wasn't the last time Bilbo wished he was home again, relaxing by his warm fireplace, about to drink a cup of hot tea. Hardly. The hobbit would repeatedly bemoan joining the quest and wish he were once again at Bag-End. You get the definite impression that Bilbo was a homebody, like many of us.

It's fine to enjoy familiar surroundings and desire familiar comforts—as long as we understand there may be times when we *can't* have them. Sometimes we're called to larger duties—like a soldier leaving home to go off to war. Second thoughts at such times are natural—but the Bible tells us, "You therefore must endure hardship as a good soldier of Jesus Christ" (2 Timothy 2:3 NKJV).

Had Mr. Baggins known just what hardships, privations, and dangers he'd have to endure, he likely wouldn't have started the journey. But for us, the Bible clearly warns that living for Christ will be difficult at times. Paul and Barnabas told the early Christians, "We must go through many hardships to enter the kingdom of God" (Acts 14:22 NIV). This was no aside. It was practically Paul's keynote address to the believers in Lystra, Iconium, and Antioch— and to us as well. Though it's written plainly in the Bible, many of us don't read it. . .or don't quite believe it applies to us today.

Despite his initial whining over the inconveniences of a rainstorm, Bilbo grew tougher through his experiences. In time, it took increasingly greater dangers and privations to cause him to bemoan his lot.

The hobbit continued to have second thoughts (and third, fourth, fifth, and sixth thoughts), as he was, after all, being tested to the limits of his endurance. But Mr. Baggins changed. He was no longer just an overfed hobbit longing for luxury and comfort. He traveled farther and farther from home to face almost unimaginable difficulties.

Of *course* he occasionally longed for the things he'd once enjoyed—but he stayed his course.

And when Bilbo finally did return home from his journey, he appreciated the singing of his teakettle more than ever before. Well, he deserved it!

Scripture talks of the great heroes of faith and describes them as "foreigners and nomads here on earth" (Hebrews 11:13 NLT)—pilgrims merely traveling through a weary world. The passage continues: "If they had longed for the country they came from, they could have gone back" (Hebrews 11:15 NLT). But though they were weary and tempted at times—nearly overwhelmed in some cases—they didn't *long* to return. They didn't set their heart on returning to their old life.

Nor did Bilbo turn around and trot back to the Shire. He was committed to the quest.

We'll need the same commitment, because we're sure to be tested. But when we're resolved not to give up, a mere lack of creature comforts won't turn us from our path. We'll remain steadfast. God himself will strengthen us.

As an ancient poet said in Psalm 84:5, "Blessed is the man whose strength is in You, whose heart is set on pilgrimage" (NKJV).

9

When God Isn't There

Not until then did they notice that Gandalf
was missing. . . . "Just when a wizard would have
been most useful, too," groaned Dori and Nori.
THE HOBBIT, CHAPTER 2

Early in the quest, Gandalf traveled with Thorin and company, talking, laughing, providing a source of cheer and reassurance. To a certain point, the adventure had been a safe and happy excursion into new lands.

Though the dwarves hadn't needed Gandalf to perform magic—yet—that thought was tucked away in the back of their minds. If the necessity arose, Gandalf would use his power to protect or rescue the group. This was, in fact, the reason Thorin had insisted Gandalf come along. The dwarf leader wouldn't have put it quite so bluntly as to say he wanted to *use* Gandalf. But in essence, that's what he wished.

Then came the dark, rainy night when the dwarves faced their first real hardship. They turned to Gandalf to find he was inexplicably missing. In a duet of misery, Dori and Nori moaned, "Just when a wizard would've been most useful, too!"

So now it was out in the open: the dwarves saw Gandalf as an insurance policy, offering 100 percent coverage to protect and rescue them from the slightest distress and discomfort. Gandalf was like their private genie—not in a bottle, of course, but riding with them on a magnificent white steed. They had brought the wizard along because. . . yes, they thought he'd be "useful."

Needing a fire to warm themselves, cook their food, and dry their clothes, even the most skilled dwarf was unable to start one because of the heavy downpour. But Gandalf had special power over fire. (In fact, though they weren't aware of it, he bore the elvish ring Narya, the Ring of Fire.)

So why had the wizard picked now, of all times, to leave the dwarves?

The children of Israel could certainly identify with the dwarves' predicament. God had promised them, "See, I am sending an angel before you to protect you on your journey and lead you safely to the place I have prepared for you" (Exodus 23:20 NLT). Now, this was no ordinary angel—he represented God Himself. Yet repeatedly, when their sufferings and privations were the most acute, God seemed to disappear. When the people were desperately thirsty or hungry, all they could see was the bleak Sinai Desert, dust clouds blowing over its rock-strewn surface.

So they complained that God had abandoned them.

Today, we face times when it seems God isn't there. We can't see Him. It doesn't *feel* like He's there. But He hasn't abandoned us. God is always there, and He hears our cries—even if, to our limited senses, He seems to have gone away or stopped listening to our prayers. As the prophet Isaiah said, "LORD, your hand is lifted high, but they do not see it" (Isaiah 26:11 NIV).

Just when Thorin and company's situation was most desperate, Gandalf *did* return and rescue them. Often, that's how it goes with us. *Why,* we wonder, *does God allow us to suffer and be tested to such extremes before He finally steps in and answers our prayers? What purpose do His silences accomplish?* Doesn't God know that such inexplicable delays frustrate us, cause us to doubt His goodness, and question that He's truly there for us?

These are difficult questions. And prepackaged answers don't help.

But there *are* answers, whether or not they're easy to digest. If we're honest, we probably admit that those really tough times in our lives—when we were tested right to the edge of our endurance—are the times when we grew the most spiritually. Hardships made us more mature or created in us a deeper empathy for the suffering of others. This is not to call them pleasant times or anything we'd care to repeat—but they were, in the end, *good* for us.

Make no mistake: The Christian life can be very difficult. Contrary to a song you may have learned in Sunday school, following Jesus won't make you "happy all the time." Jesus Himself often walked a difficult road, and we are to "live...as Jesus did" (1 John 2:6 NLT).

That sounds like bad news if you thought being a Christian meant perpetual health and wealth. But the good news is that Jesus is our shepherd—and He promised that when He takes us out of safe places and into the wild, He will personally lead the way (John 10:3–4). Jesus not only walks with us, he walks *in front of* us. We simply follow in His footsteps.

"Never will I leave you," Jesus said, "never will I forsake you" (Hebrews 13:5 NIV). However contrary our feelings may be, the Lord is always with us. Not for us to "use"—He is Lord and Master, after all—but to help us through our most difficult times.

10

Pride Goes Before a Fall

A really first-class and legendary burglar would
at this point have picked the trolls' pockets—
it is nearly always worth while.
THE HOBBIT, CHAPTER 2

U p to the time of Bilbo's adventure, hobbits hadn't pro-
duced many books. Oh, there were some—and af-
fluent families like the Bagginses were avid collectors of
these rare volumes. Sitting in the comfort of his hobbit
hole, Bilbo had read about a good many things he'd never
actually seen or done. So when the dwarves sent him to
investigate a fire and he saw three gargantuan trolls nearby,
Bilbo immediately recognized them for what they were.

He had also read up on burglars—"Expert Treasure-hunters," as the dwarf Gloin once described them. As few books as there were, Bilbo had probably read those volumes more than once. He was very familiar with the subject.

So when Gandalf explained that Bilbo—because of his ability to move absolutely silently—was to be the burglar, the hobbit readily accepted the role. It appealed to common sense: of course any job requiring stealth called for a hobbit. Hobbits have an unusual talent for being furtive. In fact, Tolkien tells us, "They take a pride in it."[12]

And Mr. Baggins had a particular issue with pride at this time.

Earlier, the dwarves had insinuated that Bilbo was no good. How insulting! As a first-class, legendary burglar, Bilbo decided to prove the dwarves wrong by picking these trolls' pockets.

Thorin and company later complained that he should've just snatched a bit of food or come back and reported the danger. But Bilbo was avenging a slight to his honor: he was out to impress the dwarves with just what a clever burglar he was when the trolls caught him. As a result, all of the dwarves were nearly killed and eaten.

"Pride goes before destruction, and a haughty spirit before a fall" (Proverbs 16:18 NKJV).

Pride caused the downfall of many Bible characters as well.

King Nebuchadnezzar, at the height of his power, boasted, "Look at this great city of Babylon! By my own mighty power, I have built this beautiful city as my royal residence to display my majestic splendor" (Daniel 4:30 NLT). No sooner had he spoken these words than he went mad as the proverbial hatter.

Nebuchadnezzar was driven from his royal residence and forced to live with wild beasts. The prophet Daniel summed up the lesson for Nebuchadnezzar's son (actually, grandson), saying, "Your Majesty, the Most High God gave your father Nebuchadnezzar sovereignty and greatness and glory and splendor. . . . But when his heart became arrogant and hardened with pride, he was deposed from his royal throne and stripped of his glory" (Daniel 5:18, 20 NIV).

Another biblical king, Uzziah, serves as an example: He was a good, godly ruler who was greatly strengthened by God. "But after Uzziah became powerful," 2 Chronicles 26:16 tells us, "his pride led to his downfall" (NIV). Uzziah began to think he was hot stuff—and right at the height of his power, he stumbled.

God has given each of us natural talents, and He wants us to use them for good and to help others. False humility—denying we're good at something when we know that we actually are—is no virtue. But, on the other hand, the apostle Paul warns, "Don't think you are better than you really are. Be honest in your evaluation of yourselves" (Romans 12:3 NLT).

The danger comes when we become overconfident of our abilities—or when we try to show off how "good" we are. Then we begin to take needless risks to impress others, setting ourselves up for a face-plant. Humility and an honest evaluation of our limitations, however, can save us from a disastrous fall.

Like Bilbo, we might occasionally *need* to fall flat on our faces to keep us from being cocky. The sooner that happens in our journey of faith, the better. Most of us have some issue of pride to wrestle with. But once we've been thrown to the mat and had our attitude corrected, an appropriately healthy sense of self-worth and an accurate knowledge of our limits will allow us to be of actual use to God and others.

Then, when the Lord puts us in situations where we shine and our talent comes to the fore, the whole thing won't go to our head. Sure, if we've done a good job, we'll know it—but we won't get puffed up with pride. We won't think we're God's gift to humanity. We'll understand we were just the right person in the right place at the right time, and we did what we had to do. That's all.

And Bilbo? Eventually, he went on to prove that he *was*, after all, a first-class burglar—and saved the dwarves from danger again and again.

11

Watch and Pray

"And what brought you back in the nick of time?"
"Looking behind," said he.
THE HOBBIT, CHAPTER 2

After Bilbo's bungled burglary, the trolls began to question whether there were other intruders nearby. Trolls aren't all that bright, but they are highly suspicious. Fortunately, they're also easily distracted.

In the middle of their interrogation, the trolls began to quarrel and were soon physically fighting each other. Hearing the racket, the dwarves crept up to see what was happening. The trolls, however, spotted the nonstealthy dwarves and deftly captured them in sacks. Then the trolls began discussing how to cook their prisoners.

Earlier that evening, Gandalf had disappeared—and the night was far spent when he returned, quiet and unseen. Quickly sizing up the situation, the wizard imitated the trolls' voices to set them arguing afresh. Gandalf's tactic got the trolls so busy insulting each other that they failed to retreat underground before sunrise. So it was that the first rays of dawn turned them to stone.

Thorin later asked the wizard where he'd gone, and Gandalf explained that he'd gone to scout ahead. When Thorin inquired what made him return just in time, Gandalf simply replied, "Looking behind."

Gandalf then shared another reason for riding ahead in the dark: He was anxious to replenish the group's small stock of provisions—and he knew there were villages nearby where they could find food. Tolkien doesn't tell us whether Gandalf arrived to find abandoned cottages, but that's what he would have seen: The trolls boasted that they'd recently eaten a village and a half among them, and Gandalf met two elves—themselves hurrying along for fear of the trolls—who said the rest of the villagers had fled in terror.

With the elves' information, Gandalf had felt an immediate concern that Thorin's company was in danger. As soon as he'd seen the fire, he'd rushed toward it.

Gandalf's sensation may seem mystical to us—but God often warns people when they or their loved ones face danger. Such warnings may be like the "still, small voice" that Elijah heard (1 Kings 19:12 KJV). And though it's usually an urgent prompting, it may not be an audible voice speaking distinct words. God simply impresses on believers' hearts that danger is imminent—and they need to act immediately.

Then again, God doesn't *always* work this way. More often than not, the onus is on us to be alert and understand the significance of things we see and hear. Solomon admonished, "A prudent person foresees danger and takes precautions" (Proverbs 27:12 NLT). So we can heed the warnings of the Holy Spirit—if that's how God chooses to communicate with us—*and* have our heads about us, astutely judging the situations we experience.

As Jesus Himself said, "Watch and pray" (Mark 14:38 NLT).

As with much of the Christian life, we need to find the proper balance. We're not to be so spiritually minded that we ignore the plain evidence of our senses. On the other hand, we can't depend just on what our eyes and ears tell us. After all, "There is a way that seems right to a man, but its end is the way of death" (Proverbs 14:12 NKJV). Sometimes, though we can't explain why, we simply *know* something is wrong. We're uneasy and can't shake the feeling. What we call a "gut feeling," however, is often God's Spirit speaking to our heart (not our stomach) that something is amiss.

Whether we know exactly why we feel that way, we feel strongly that our help is needed. Is that some intuition that our loved ones are in danger, or are we simply motivated by a general concern? We may never know. Very likely, it's a combination of the two. We know that if there's even the slightest chance that our friends or family are in any kind of trouble—some immediate danger or just difficult times—we want to be there for them.

The most important thing is that we love and care for others, so that when we *do* get a feeling that they need our help, we don't shrug it off and go casually about our own business. Maybe we'll drop in on them. We'll make a phone call or send an e-mail.

Will this sometimes mean answering a false alarm? Yes—but so be it. Better to be like the parents who pace the driveway, cell phone in hand, breathing a sigh of relief as their errant child rides up the street half an hour late, than to be completely unconcerned. Better to realize that we worried needlessly. At least it's proof of our love.

12

God Is in the Details

"Would this be any good?" asked Bilbo. . . .
"I found it on the ground where the trolls
had their fight." He held out a largish key.
THE HOBBIT, CHAPTER 2

After coming down from the mountains, the three trolls—William, Bert, and Tom—had pillaged villages near Rivendell. They finally settled in the woods not far from the road, and from there they waylaid travelers.

The trolls chose this spot for a reason: They can't bear sunlight, which turns them into stone. Staying awake all night—on the graveyard shift, so to speak—they hide during the day in a cave or hole. But right here William, Bert, and Tom had discovered a cave with a stone door. It was the perfect hidey-hole.

The cave, as it turned out, was an ancient treasure trove, complete with a key to unlock the door. (Now, what are the odds of *that*?) William, as leader, kept the key in his pocket. But after catching Bilbo, he and Bert began fighting like dogs, rolling on the ground, kicking and pounding each other. And the key tumbled out of his pocket.

Now, with the trolls turned to stone, Thorin and company were safe. But the dwarves and Bilbo still had no food. So Gandalf reminded them that the trolls must have had a cave nearby.

After a careful search, they did find a stone door in the side of the hill—but no matter what they did, they couldn't open it. Soon the dwarves were exhausted and cross.

That's when Bilbo held up the key and asked, "Would this be any good?" Gandalf snatched the key, inserted it in the keyhole, and opened the door. Inside, the travelers found not only food to eat, but pots of gold coins and several swords. The food filled their bellies and the coins provided wealth. Two of the swords in particular proved to be extremely valuable.

A key is such a small thing. And the Bible asks, "Who has despised the day of small things?" (Zechariah 4:10 NKJV)

The answer, unfortunately, is that *most* of us have at one time or another despised small things. Yet those things are often the key to solving the larger problems that beset us. Sometimes we literally need a key—we've probably all locked ourselves out of our house or car at some time. And if you've ever forgotten the password to your e-mail account or couldn't remember the PIN for your bank card, you know the frustration of being unable to get the information or money you desperately need.

We can't be held responsible if our keys get lost while trolls battle—but as we all know, that's usually *not* how things are misplaced. Important items go missing because we're in a hurry, or we don't pay enough attention to put them in their proper place. (You don't want to get in the way of a scatterbrained person heading out to shop but frantically looking for a misplaced bank card.)

Some people are so meticulous and methodical that they almost never have this problem. Good for them. But even the best-organized people can misplace things. Then even *they* get down on the floor to search, look through dresser drawers, and turn pockets inside-out trying to figure out just where "it" is.

But perhaps the worst thing is to look and look for a lost item, only to realize later that it was in front of us the whole time.

That can happen with the "keys" of scripture: Sometimes we wonder what to do in a new or perplexing situation, only to kick ourselves later—*after* we've mishandled things—when we learn that the Bible speaks clearly on that very subject and situation. Yet many of us, because of a lack of knowledge of even the most basic scriptures, fail to do the right thing at the right time. Even if we're vaguely aware that a certain verse says something along the lines of such-and-such, we don't remember *exactly* what it says—and often have no clue where in the Bible it can be found.

Jesus promised, "The Holy Spirit, whom the Father will send in my name, will teach you all things and will remind you of everything I have said to you" (John 14:26 NIV). The Holy Spirit longs to remind us what God's Word says—but we need to *read* the Bible in the first place to learn what Jesus said.

As we read scripture, we may wonder, *How does this apply today?* That's fine—if we turn that question into a prayer, God can provide answers for everyday living, even for the most complex situations.

Don't despise the "day of small things." Small things are often the keys to vast treasures.

13

The Sword of the Spirit

"These look like good blades," said the wizard, half drawing
them and looking at them curiously. "They were not
made by any troll, nor by any smith among men."
THE HOBBIT, CHAPTER 2

Among the treasures in the troll cave were swords of various makes, sizes, and designs. Because of their exquisitely crafted scabbards and jewel-encrusted hilts, two in particular attracted the attention of Gandalf and Thorin. Wise as he was, not even Gandalf knew about the swords—though he noted they seemed to be good blades. Just how good he would find out later.

Gandalf took one sword; Thorin claimed the other.

Bilbo picked out a knife in a common leather sheath. For the diminutive hobbit, it was like a short sword.

After the group arrived in Rivendell, Elrond looked over the weapons and provided an idea of their true worth: The swords had been made by the High Elves in the fabled city of Gondolin. Runes on Thorin's sword indicated its name was *Orcrist* ("the Goblin-cleaver"), while the markings on Gandalf's sword named it *Glamdring* ("Foe-hammer"). It had once belonged to Turgon, king of Gondolin.

When goblins later captured Thorin and company, they recognized the swords and let out howls of rage. Small wonder! These swords had slain many goblins, burning with a blue flame when goblins were near. Gandalf's sword later "made no trouble whatever of cutting through the goblin-chains and setting all the prisoners free."[13]

Bilbo's blade was also of elvish make and, though much smaller, had incredible powers as well. It, too, gleamed with a blue light when goblins were at hand. Years later, Bilbo gave it to Frodo, and in a desperate act of courage, Frodo used it to pierce the stony hide of a troll in the Mines of Moria. (Boromir, wielding the sharpest, strongest blade of Gondor with all his strength, only succeeded in denting his blade on the monster.)[14]

Wouldn't it be great if such amazing weapons actually existed?

In a very real sense, they do—though not in our physical dimension. The Bible often talks of powerful spirits, particularly angels, armed with swords (see Joshua 5:13–14). While some people view such spiritual weapons as metaphorical, others believe the battles in the spiritual realm involve very real, albeit supernatural, weapons wielded by angels and demons. Literal or symbolic? You decide. Either way, these weapons pack a lot of power.

Would you be surprised to learn that we mortals have access to a sword not made by "any smith among men"? The apostle Paul urged us to take "the sword of the Spirit, which is the word of God" (Ephesians 6:17 NKJV). And just as Glamdring had no trouble slicing through goblin chains, so the sword of the Spirit can cut the figurative chains that bind the human spirit. "The word of God is living and powerful, and sharper than any two-edged sword," the Bible says, "and is a discerner of the thoughts and intents of the heart" (Hebrews 4:12 NKJV). Scriptures don't glow with a blue light when evil is near—but they are certainly a spiritual light. By reading them, we understand how to discern between good and evil.

This parallel—between God's Word and a supernatural sword—is neither casual nor accidental. God fully intended it as a picture that we could understand. No doubt, the recurrent theme of powerful, mystical swords in fantasy novels originates with this imagery in the Bible. Fantastic swords of fantasy stories are, clearly, fantasy—but the sword of the Spirit is real and actually has great power.

At a glance, you'd scarcely suspect that God's Word has that much power. Sure—like the elvish swords that appeared to be important heirlooms, many people respect the Bible as a valuable book of fascinating stories and enlightened moral principles. But do they know of its life-changing power? God's Word tells us how to find eternal life by believing in Jesus, but it doesn't stop there—it gives us power to stand strong in *this* life also.

Along with faith and earnest prayer, the Bible is one of the most powerful weapons we have. In the Bible, God has made many promises to us (see 2 Peter 1:4). During times of spiritual testing or desperate need, we wield the sword of the Spirit by reading and meditating on these promises, asking God to fulfill them in our lives.

And there's even more. God's word is far more powerful than our own reasoning, as the apostle Paul wrote to Christians in Corinth: "We use God's mighty weapons, not worldly weapons, to knock down the strongholds of human reasoning and to destroy false arguments" (2 Corinthians 10:4 NLT). When Paul shared the gospel or tried to convince people that what he was saying was true, he didn't rely on his own oratory. He quoted the scriptures.

He wielded the sword of the Spirit.

May we, too, realize the great power of God's Word—and learn how to use it.

14

The Road to Rivendell

The only path was marked with white stones, some of which were small, and others were half covered with moss or heather.
THE HOBBIT, CHAPTER 3

Leaving the troll's cave, Gandalf led Thorin and company east toward the elven refuge of Rivendell. The forests dropped away behind them; ahead the semi-barren terrain was "a wide land the colour of heather and crumbling rock,"[15] one vast slope gradually rising toward the Misty Mountains in the distance. The landscape was seemingly uniform, with no warning even of approaching streams. Suddenly, to the travelers' surprise, steep chasms would appear in the ground in front of them.

Then there were treacherous bogs that appeared to be solid ground, festooned with lovely flowers—yet if a horse and rider ventured in, they'd never return alive.

This land was a deceptively vast and bewildering terrain of unending sameness—a place to easily get lost. The group was nearing Rivendell, but none could tell just where it was. The road they'd been following had petered out, and the faint path that remained was marked with white stones. The stones, however, were often quite small and hard to see—or half-covered with moss and heather.

Having been to Rivendell many times before, Gandalf knew the way as well as anyone could. But even with the wizard as guide, the going was slow. To make matters even more difficult, daylight was rapidly fading. In the darkness, the ponies began to stumble on stones.

On the verge of a hidden haven, it looked as if Gandalf and his team would have to camp in the barren-lands that night. But then. . .just before total darkness engulfed the land, the travelers came to a river valley. In the distance below, they saw a light. Rivendell at last!

Ever have such an experience?

We long to reach our goals; we yearn to stay on track to success—but our way is not plainly marked. We're often perplexed and bewildered and wander off our path. Like Bilbo and the dwarves—or Christian in *Pilgrim's Progress*—

we must carefully pick our way through the treacherous terrain, avoiding the Swamp of Despair and the dark pits that we could fall into.

Only rarely has God told people exactly which road to walk, whom they'd meet, and what would happen when they met them. But He certainly can. Back in Bible times, God told Saul to travel to a tomb at Zelzah, on the border of Benjamin, where he'd meet two men. They would tell Saul that his father was looking for him. Saul was then to go to the great tree of Tabor, where he'd meet three men en route to Bethel; these men would offer him some bread. After that, Saul would go to Gibeah, and just outside the town he'd meet a company of prophets playing musical instruments. And all these things happened! (See 1 Samuel 10:1–9.)

Now *that's* the kind of direction we'd like—every day, thank you very much. Most of us want to see the big picture and all the details, preferably in high definition. Like King David prayed, "Cause me to know the way in which I should walk" (Psalm 143:8 NKJV).

But, as another psalm writer noted, "Thy word is a lamp unto my feet, and a light unto my path" (Psalm 119:105 KJV). The picture is of a small clay lamp that sheds a flickering light, only enough to illuminate the ground immediately ahead. God usually guides us step-by-step—

not with floodlights bathing the entire landscape, alerting us to every possible pitfall. He rarely hands us a day's itinerary ahead of time. Rather, God shows us where to place our feet, one step at a time, while we travel.

How many of us are happy to stumble toward our goal through a confusing, mazelike landscape in near darkness? But, frequently, that's just the way life is. We have just enough light and wisdom to see the path immediately ahead. . .if we look hard.

Why doesn't God make things easier for us? Doesn't He know that we're trying our best to follow Him? Surely He hears us when we pray for His will, and He knows we need as many large, clear signs as possible to keep us on the right path.

Well, yes—God does know. And in ethical and moral matters He's given us very clear guidelines so we don't have to go astray. But He has *not* handed down specific guidelines for every detail of our daily lives—such as where to find the nearest parking spot, how to locate the best bargains, or even how to make the best career choice.

God generally provides markers and indications— often faint and semi-obscured—like the small white stones on the road to Rivendell. To find them takes some diligent searching. But He knows it's best to keep us on a short leash, close to Him.

Is it difficult to follow God and determine His will? Yes, indeed. But He will always supply just enough light and wisdom for our particular path.

15

Taking Counsel with the Wise

*He thought their opinion of his adventure
might be interesting. Elves know a lot
and are wondrous folk for news.*
THE HOBBIT, CHAPTER 3

Of all the races that inhabited Middle-earth, elves were
the firstborn. They were the elder children of Eru
(God); men were the younger. Elves were similar to man-
kind in its original, unfallen state—very fair and immortal.
(Elves weren't exactly immortal but just about.)

Elrond, the lord of Rivendell, had been born in the
First Age and was well over six thousand years old at the
time Bilbo met him. He had seen a great many events over

the millennia and was, as a result, both profoundly sadder and immensely wiser.

Bilbo had, on rare occasions, met elves passing through the Shire, and though he was somewhat afraid of them, he was also keenly interested in elf-lore. He'd often surprise his fellow hobbits with statements such as, "It's the Elves' New Year tomorrow!"[16] Now that Bilbo was actually *among* elves, he wanted to talk with them and ask questions—especially regarding the quest he was on. Having already traveled far beyond the borders of anything he'd experienced before, Bilbo was plodding relentlessly toward danger. It was a prime time to get counsel from the wise!

Who wouldn't jump at the chance to talk with someone more than *sixty centuries* old? Wouldn't you respect the wisdom of a venerable old-timer who had witnessed the rise and fall of kings more often than you've turned the pages on a calendar?

The Bible tells us: "With the ancient is wisdom; and in the length of days understanding" (Job 12:12 KJV). Of course, the wise ancients we know are not millennia old. Nor are they eternally youthful and fair. They are gray-haired, wrinkled, and often forgetful. Some of their fingers are gnarled, and some of their teeth may be missing. Yet if we are to gain wise counsel, it is to these seasoned mentors that we must turn.

"Without counsel, plans go awry, but in the multitude of counselors they are established" (Proverbs 15:22 NKJV). Anyone can give advice, and young people can at times inform us wisely. But as a rule, a multitude of years provides both experience and wisdom—and we ignore the advice of the aged at our peril.

A classic example is the young king Rehoboam. After his father Solomon's death, the people of Israel asked Rehoboam to ease up on them, lowering their exorbitantly high taxes. Rehoboam first turned for advice to the old men who had served his father. The elders wisely responded that if Rehoboam would treat the people fairly and kindly, they'd be his loyal subjects forever. Seeking a second opinion, however, Rehoboam turned to the young men who'd been raised with him in the palace. They witlessly told Rehoboam to assert himself, show the people who was boss, and tell them he was going to be even more demanding than his father had been.

No big surprise: most of the kingdom revolted (see 1 Kings 12:1–17).

The young are usually full of self-confidence, with grand dreams and ambitions. Up to a certain age, we believe that all of our plans will work. Many of our peers advise enthusiastically, "Go for it!" That advice may be encouraging and what we *want* to hear—but it's in our own best interests to seek the experience and wisdom of those who have lived life with all its ups and downs, successes and failures. If we listen carefully to these older, wiser folks, we can avoid the pitfalls our own exuberance might plunge us into.

Resist the assumption that older people are out of touch with today's world—that their hard-earned wisdom is not relevant to our modern situations. The temptation is to wonder what they could possibly tell us about relationship problems or career choices when they haven't the first clue about how to send a text message or change the settings on a computer. Never confuse knowledge—especially of technical things—with wisdom.

Bilbo, Gandalf, and the dwarves sought counsel from Elrond because he was well versed in ancient lore and had specific knowledge of the path ahead. As a result, "Their plans were improved with the best advice."[17] Note: It wasn't just any advice, but the *best* advice available. We do well, when making plans or embarking on a journey, to seek the wisdom of those who have walked the road years before us. They will have a clear idea of what we're up against.

An interesting side note to all of this: While Bilbo, Gandalf, and Thorin were counseling with Elrond, there was an eleven-year-old lad living in Rivendell. Named Estel, this ward of Elrond would grow to manhood, assume his rightful name of Aragorn, and become king of Gondor.[18] Aragorn's wisdom to rule derived in large part from his upbringing by Elrond.

16

Someone Has to Do It

*"The summer is getting on down below," thought
Bilbo, "and haymaking is going on and picnics.
They will be harvesting and blackberrying."*
THE HOBBIT, CHAPTER 4

Having left Rivendell, Thorin and company began their ascent of the Misty Mountains. Plodding steadily upward, climbing the mountains' treacherous flanks day after weary day, they met no other travelers on the way. The higher they climbed, the colder it became—and soon the wind was shrieking among the rocks. Several times, boulders broke loose, bounding toward them, passing perilously close by.

After a time, Bilbo turned to look over the landscape spread out behind him. Though he couldn't make out the Shire in the distance, Bilbo knew that it was a busy, happy time for the hobbits back home. *Home!* He was missing not only the comfort and convenience of his own little kitchen but everything familiar and enjoyable that he'd left behind.

Tolkien describes the richness of a Shire autumn: "The trees were laden with apples, honey was dripping in the combs, and the corn was tall and full."[19] Autumn was a choice time of year for hobbits, filled with rich harvests, haymaking—and doubtless hayrides. It was a time for picking sweet, ripe blackberries and making them into delicious pies and jams. It was a time for picnics, feasting, and merrymaking in the peaceful setting of the Shire. For Bilbo—ever the generous host and lover of parties and food—autumn must have been an especially happy time.

But Bilbo had left all that behind. And inside was the niggling anxiety that he might, as Thorin had warned, never return. For a hobbit, this was a heavy load to bear.

Sometimes we make choices that bring a heavy load on us while life is, relatively speaking, a picnic for others. Maybe we've committed to helping the elderly and the disadvantaged, or to volunteering in our church. We do these things because we know they're right, because we feel called to them. Sometimes we step up to the plate simply because no one else has. *Someone* has to do it, after all.

At first, we can give ourselves wholeheartedly to the task, buoyed by our idealism and Christian love. But there come times when we begin to miss our free time—relaxing with a book, talking on the phone, watching a movie with our friends. Walking a difficult road in the company of near strangers, we can almost hear the laughter and see the happy faces of those still enjoying what we're now missing.

Bilbo knew his quest was important, but he had no idea *how* important. Gandalf hadn't gone into great detail about recovering the dwarves' treasure. Left unsaid was the truth that Smaug himself would have to be slain. With Sauron rising again to rebuild his empire, Gandalf was deeply concerned that the Dark Lord would join forces with the dragon. Then the north—and eventually the Shire and all of Middle-earth—would be in peril. As Bilbo's nephew Frodo said many years later, when the things one holds dear are in peril, "some one has to give them up, lose them, so that others may keep them."[20]

Jesus Himself had a home for about the first thirty years of His life—and even after His public ministry began, He enjoyed food and friendship in the homes of people such as Mary and Martha. But Jesus was very often on the road. He *had* to be. He had to give up his own comfortable dwelling to travel around Israel, sharing God's good news with others. "Now it happened as they journeyed on the road, that someone said to him, 'Lord, I will follow You wherever You go.' And Jesus said to him, 'Foxes have holes and birds of the air have nests, but the Son of Man has nowhere to lay His head'" (Luke 9:57–58 NKJV).

Like Gandalf, God often seeks people for important jobs. And those jobs frequently involve a relinquishing of comforts we've become accustomed to. As a result, there's often a shortage of volunteers.

If we've said yes to God's invitation, however, it's essential that we stick to the task—even though we know others are relaxing and enjoying themselves while we're walking a lonely, difficult road. Mind you, the things those others are enjoying aren't necessarily bad or wrong. They may be the well-earned fruits of their labor.

But in those times that God calls us apart for a special mission, we may have to give up some comforts, some friends, even some of our family relationships. Are you on the road with Jesus right now? If not, enjoy your rest— because He may call you up for service soon!

17

Checking Things Out

"Have you thoroughly explored it?" said the wizard, who knew that caves up in the mountains were seldom unoccupied.
THE HOBBIT, CHAPTER 4

One night, as the travelers huddled under a narrow ledge near the top of the mountain range, a terrific thunderstorm broke loose. Rain came down in sheets, drenching the group, and lightning bolts struck the side of the mountain, shattering rocks. And if that weren't bad enough, stone-giants added to the general mayhem by hurling boulders back and forth in the storm.

Thorin had finally had enough, so he sent the two youngest dwarves—Fili and Kili—on ahead to look for a better shelter. Not long afterward, they returned. Yes, they'd found a dry cave.

"Have you thoroughly explored it?" Gandalf asked. They assured him they had, so the travelers and their ponies made their way there. Using the light atop his staff, Gandalf then thoroughly searched the entire cave himself. Nothing seemed amiss, so they settled in and were soon fast asleep. In the dead of the night, however, a secret door in the back opened, and hordes of goblins rushed out, seized the travelers and their ponies, and vanished back inside the mountain.

Gandalf and Elrond knew that "most of the passes were infested by evil things and dreadful dangers,"[21] particularly orcs (another name for goblins). That's why they had advised Thorin and company to take *this* pass. Since it was a higher, more precipitous passage, no orcs had previously lurked there. The goblins' main gate overlooked a lower, easier pass where they'd caught many travelers, but word had gotten out, and people stopped going that way. Realizing that their former trap was now known, the goblins opened this new entrance to ambush travelers. This was so recent that neither Gandalf nor Elrond were aware of it.

Our world today is also full of hidden snares that, like Venus flytraps or concealed pits, wait to trap the unwary. For example, there is the used-car salesman who sells you what appears to be a like-new car, and you only find out later that it had sat for a week under floodwaters.

Some frauds are so obvious that almost anyone can spot them, while others are so clever that the average person doesn't pick up on them. Some schemes are so complex they can withstand the scrutiny even of an expert who knows what to look for.

When these schemes are discovered and exposed, and people stop falling for them, the fraudsters simply close down shop and set up operations somewhere else. For example, you may have been warned not to believe an e-mail from a third-world country promising you that millions of dollars are waiting to be delivered to your bank account—if you'll just send back your account information and a "small" processing fee. But what if the e-mail originates from a "developed" country—say, Switzerland—instead?

Con artists lurk not only in the financial world but also in religious settings. Jesus likened these deceivers to wolves in sheep's clothing (Matthew 7:15), and Paul cautioned Christians not to be "tossed to and fro, and carried about with every wind of doctrine, by the sleight of men, and cunning craftiness, whereby they lie in wait to deceive" (Ephesians 4:14 KJV). The biblical warnings are clear: not all people who speak to us are good-hearted, but some, like trapdoor spiders, lie in wait to deceive.

So that we don't accidentally camp on the doorstep of deception and end up caught in a trap, it's incumbent upon each of us to check things out and to ask questions. For example, we would do well to check with trustworthy experts before sinking our money in a financial scheme that seems too good to be true. (It usually is!) Likewise, we should check with trusted pastors and Christian friends before opening our sails and allowing ourselves to be blown about by some exciting new "wind of doctrine."

Sometimes, however, only God can forewarn us or steer us away from carefully disguised traps that (at least at first) are capable of fooling even the veterans. And once we've escaped a scam or a deception ourselves, we have an obligation to warn *others* to watch out for it.

Gandalf decided to take this one step further: after their escape, he was already making plans to enlist the help of a giant to block the goblins' secret entrance with stones.

In addition, the Bible warns not to take advantage of others' ignorance and sell them a bum steer. That's defrauding. And when someone tries to sell us something, we're not to claim that it's worthless junk so we can get it dirt cheap. The following proverb sums that up: "'It's no good, it's no good!' says the buyer—then goes off and boasts about the purchase" (Proverbs 20:14 NIV). Ultimately, the Bible warns, such deception will backfire on you. "If you set a trap for others, you will get caught in it yourself" (Proverbs 26:27 NLT)—not always right away but over time.

Buyer beware! And seller take care.

18

The Goblins' Return

*Dwarves had not passed that way for many years. . .
and the goblins had spread in secret after
the battle of the Mines of Moria.*
THE HOBBIT, CHAPTER 4

In ages past, Thorin's clan had discovered great riches in
the mines of Moria, deep under the Misty Mountains,
and had become exceedingly prosperous. But in their greed
to discover the precious metal *mithril*, they had dug too
deep. They awakened a Balrog—a gigantic demon—and
were forced to flee. Many of them went north to Lonely
Mountain, but then Smaug drove the dwarves from
there, too.

Twenty years later, Thorin's grandfather, Thror, set off to seek his fortune, but instead of returning to Lonely Mountain, he went to Moria. In the dwarves' long absence, orcs had occupied Moria, and Azog the orc chief beheaded Thror. Outraged, Thorin's father summoned all the dwarf clans together to avenge this evil. The War of the Dwarves and Orcs began in 2793 T.A., and after six years of bitter battles the dwarves succeeded in driving the goblins completely out of the Misty Mountains. The Battle of the Mines of Moria in 2799 T.A. was the war's last bloody conflict, and Thorin himself fought there.[22]

This was now 142 years ago, and that's what Thorin referred to when he said, "We have long ago paid the goblins of Moria."[23] As far as he was concerned, that war was *long* over. Thorin was unaware that in the years since, goblins had secretly spread back into the Misty Mountains. Now, as orcs chained the dwarves together and marched them down into the bowels of the mountain, Thorin was probably thinking, *Man! I thought we got rid of these guys!* Indeed they had, but new goblins were back. And now they dragged the dwarves before the Great Goblin to decide whether to enslave them, eat them, or imprison them in snake-pits.

Most of us have fought our share of "goblin wars" in years past—perhaps even recently. These are our struggles against personal demons, whether real or figurative. When we first put our faith in Jesus and trusted Him to save us, we knew we needed to turn from our old way of life and allow God's Spirit to change us. As the Bible says, "Since you have heard about Jesus and have learned the truth that comes from him, throw off your old sinful nature and your former way of life, which is corrupted by lust and deception. Instead, let the Spirit renew your thoughts and attitudes" (Ephesians 4:21–23 NLT).

Letting God renew our attitudes was easy in *some* cases—but when it came to entrenched habits, change sometimes involved a protracted battle. Still, we were desperate to clean house of vices such as greed, lust, pornography, alcoholism, and other addictions; pride; or any one of a number of besetting sins. Our long battle was not without setbacks and failures, but in the end, because we earnestly desired to please God—and because we couldn't stand our old habits any longer—we persevered and overcame.

The danger, however, can come when we think the battles we fought when we first came to Jesus are the only ones we'll ever have to fight as Christians. What? You thought that when you were saved you became *perfect*, that you'd never have to struggle against sin again? Even the apostle Paul didn't count himself a sinless wonder. He wrote, "Not that I have already. . .arrived at my goal, but I press on to take hold of that for which Christ Jesus took hold of me. Brothers and sisters, I do not consider myself yet to have taken hold of it" (Philippians 3:12–13 NIV).

You may be victorious now in major areas of your life—and thank God for that!—but if you become self-satisfied and complacent, you may fail to see *new* goblins popping up. For example, say you used to have a problem with alcohol, but now that's history. Yes, that was a biggie, but you can't afford to look back at that major milestone in your life while failing to pay attention to the *present* goblins—goblins of jealousy, of a critical spirit, or of lust—that are creeping in *now*.

Or maybe the "new" goblins were always there, just overshadowed by the bigger, more obvious vices. Say you were a chain-smoker, and after a prolonged struggle you overcame your nicotine addiction. Now you may find that you have to deal with anger—an issue smoking used to conceal.

Like Thorin, we may wonder, "Didn't I already *win* the war against the goblins? Where did *these* guys come from?" Surprise, surprise! There are still goblins to battle. So let's stay vigilant. When it's time for a new battle, "let us cast off the works of darkness, and let us put on the armor of light" (Romans 13:12 NKJV). It takes concerted effort to strip off the remaining "works of darkness" we're still wearing, but the good news is that if we set our hearts on ditching bad habits, God will mightily help us.

19
Of Wizards and Magic

He followed after the drivers and prisoners right to
the edge of the great hall, and there he sat down and
worked up the best magic he could in the shadows.
THE HOBBIT, CHAPTER 6

When the orcs captured Thorin and company and
took them down to their cavern, Gandalf didn't
abandon them but followed, unnoticed. Then, sitting in the
shadows, he caused all the torches in the cave to go out.
Fwoosh! The great central fire vanished in thick smoke, and
sparks rained down upon the goblins. In utter darkness,
with the guards terrified, Gandalf slew the Great Goblin then urged Bilbo and the dwarves to follow him to

freedom. (This all sounds so quick and easy, but we can be sure that it *wasn't*. . .even for a wizard!)

In *The Hobbit*, Tolkien frequently refers to Gandalf as a wizard. Gandalf performed magic, cast spells, and worked bewitchments—just like all the other amusing (but quite pagan) wizards in children's tales. Had Tolkien left it at that, Gandalf would have been troubling for many Christians. Tolkien, however, decided to reconcile this with his faith. He accomplished this by rooting Gandalf firmly in the grand worldview of Middle-earth.

Gandalf, Tolkien revealed, was an exalted being called a Maia. Eru, the one God, had created the Maiar (plural of Maia) at the beginning of time. They were helpers of the Valar, the greatest spiritual beings in the Undying Lands. When the Valar became concerned about the rise of Sauron, they sent an order of Istari—Gandalf and four other Maiar—to Middle-earth. When the Istari arrived, they were in the form of old men carrying staffs. The Istari weren't actually "wizards," however. They weren't even men. They hadn't studied books to learn magic, hadn't memorized spells and incantations, nor did they tap into the power of pagan spirits to perform their magic. Their "magic" was the natural powers Eru had given them.

The Istari were strikingly similar to the angels of the Bible, and Tolkien meant it so. He said about Gandalf, "I wd. venture to say that he was an *incarnate* 'angel.'"[24]

Several times in the Old Testament, the Angel of the Lord appeared as a man carrying a staff and performed wonders. When the Angel appeared to Gideon, the prophet offered him meat and bread, setting them upon a rock: "Then the Angel of the Lord put out the end of the staff that was in his hand. . .and fire rose out of the rock and consumed the meat and the unleavened bread." Later the Angel appeared to Manoah: "And He did a wondrous thing while Manoah and his wife looked on—it happened as the flame went up toward heaven from the altar—the Angel of the Lord ascended in the flame of the altar!" (Judges 6:21; 13:19–20 NKJV).

People in Bible times definitely believed in angels. After all, these powerful spiritual beings had walked among them for thousands of years.

But what about today? Does God care enough about us to send angels among us to help us in *our* long struggles against evil? Sometimes it doesn't seem like it, but the answer is a clear "yes." Although we usually can't see them, the angels of God are constantly with us. They're not visible because, obviously, they have the power to keep mortal eyes from seeing them. And when they *are* visible, they're usually in the guise of ordinary people.

When two angels visited Lot in the city of Sodom, he

thought they were ordinary men and hospitably took them into his house. Only when a mob attacked them did the angels reveal their identity by blinding the attackers (Genesis 19:1–11).

The book of Hebrews advises us: "Don't forget to show hospitality to strangers, for some who have done this have entertained angels without realizing it!" (Hebrews 13:2 NLT).

There is another striking parallel between Tolkien's Istari and biblical angels: Only rarely did Gandalf openly use his powers. Tolkien tells us the Istari were instructed not to dominate men or to do the job for them. Rather, their mandate was to encourage and advise the Free Peoples of Middle-earth to strengthen their resolve in their long fight against evil.[25] Likewise, the main focus of the angels of God was and is to encourage and strengthen believers. They even helped Jesus. When He was in the wilderness, being tempted by Satan, "angels attended him," and when He prayed in Gethsemane, "an angel from heaven appeared to him and strengthened him" (Mark 1:13; Luke 22:43 NIV).

Angels may not often appear to us today, but they're with us in our moments of greatest need and deepest despair, speaking words of hope and encouragement to our spirits. When the apostle Paul was on a ship during a terrible, unending storm, and it looked like all was lost, an angel stood beside him and encouraged him not to give up, saying, "Do not be afraid, Paul" (Acts 27:24 NIV).

Angels still stand beside us in our darkest hour and whisper, "Do not be afraid."

20
Looking for a Way Out

I do not know how long he kept on like this, hating to go on,
not daring to stop, on, on, until he was tireder than tired.
THE HOBBIT, CHAPTER 5

After rushing Bilbo and the dwarves from the goblin
cavern, Gandalf led them down a long passageway.
He knew a way out called the Back Door, and he now
headed for it. But before they could reach freedom, the
orcs caught up to them and attacked. A dwarf named Dori
had been carrying Bilbo on his back, and when a goblin
pulled them backward, the hobbit's head hit a rock, knocking him unconscious.

Bilbo lay out of sight in a corner for a long time, and

when he came to, he was alone. There were no orcs around, but Gandalf and the dwarves were gone, too. At first, Bilbo crawled along in the pitch black; then his hand touched a small ring on the floor of the tunnel. Bilbo had no immediate use for it but put it in his pocket. Then he sat down in the stygian darkness and gave in to deep despair. He was alone—abandoned and trapped in a terrifying place with little hope of finding a way out.

Bilbo finally decided to keep walking the way Gandalf had been leading them. He couldn't see a thing, so, walking slowly with his hand feeling the wall, he continued down the passageway, avoiding turning into smaller side-branches. He went down, down, down. It seemed to Mr. Baggins as though the tunnel would never end, and he began to feel "tireder than tired."

This was not just physical weariness but exhaustion brought on by despair and fear.

Down through the ages, people have suffered times when their very spirit was drained out of them. The prophet Ezekiel wrote of a day when enemy hordes were about to sweep over the land of Israel, "When it comes, every heart will melt, all hands will be feeble, every spirit will faint, and all knees will be weak as water" (Ezekiel 21:7 NKJV).

If you are tempted to think God doesn't know how utterly down and discouraged you feel sometimes—think again. He knows what goes through your mind when you believe you've been completely abandoned, when your spirit is ready to faint, and when you want to just collapse beside the road.

You may sometimes feel trapped in a difficult situation with no way out. Perhaps you feel boxed into a deteriorating relationship you think will never get better. Or maybe you despair that you'll never finish an overwhelming assignment. Or you numbly go through the motions in a dead-end job with no Back Door leading out. Or you worry over your finances because your security has been taken away and the high hopes that once sustained you have been dashed.

Perhaps those who once showed you the way are nowhere to be found. Friends have left you or are in no position to help you. Everyone has moved on, and you feel utterly alone.

You cry out to God, but there's no answer. Deep in your heart you know He would never abandon you—but at the moment, you are walking through "the valley of the shadow of death," and it seems very much like God *has* deserted you. You continue to pray, but your prayers seem to come back unanswered. It's one thing to feel that friends and family have abandoned you, but it's quite another to feel that God Himself no longer cares.

You begin to feel a rising panic. You want to give up, but something inside you refuses to let that happen. So you battle despair, knowing that you dare not succumb to it. Like Bilbo, you continue to put one weary foot in front of the other and to walk the only direction you know.

Yes, you're walking through "the valley of the shadow of death," but that is only *half* the truth—and you can't reach the light at the end if you follow half-truths. The *full* truth is this: "Though I walk through the valley of the shadow of death, I will fear no evil; for You are with me" (Psalm 23:4 NKJV). Yes, not only is God with you right now, at this very moment, but He has also said, "Never will I leave you; never will I forsake you" (Hebrews 13:5 NIV).

God will *never* leave you—He will never, *ever* forsake you.

This is good news indeed. As the prophet wrote centuries ago, "With this news, strengthen those who have tired hands, and encourage those who have weak knees. Say to those with fearful hearts, 'Be strong, and do not fear, for your God is coming. . .to save you'" (Isaiah 35:3–4 NLT).

When you find yourself in a dark place, looking for a way out but seemingly with little hope of finding it, don't give up. If you keep praying and persevering, you'll make it. With God Himself hovering over you—His Spirit in your very heart—you will eventually emerge from your deep valley.

21

Compassion for the Fallen

*A sudden understanding, a pity mixed
with horror, welled up in Bilbo's heart.*
THE HOBBIT, CHAPTER 5

When Bilbo stepped into the edge of a dark, cold subterranean lake, he knew he could go no farther. The hobbit soon realized that *something* lived down there—Gollum, a scrawny, slimy creature with bulbous, glowing eyes. Long centuries ago, Gollum had been a hobbit named Sméagol, but he'd been overcome by the power of a magic ring and was now a desperate shadow of his former self.

Gollum would have strangled and eaten Bilbo, but,

fortunately, he wasn't hungry at the moment. Plus, Mr. Baggins had a sword. Gollum, therefore, challenged Bilbo to a riddle game. When Bilbo won, he insisted that Gollum show him the way out. That's when Gollum realized he'd lost his magic ring and let out an anguished cry. The hobbit didn't know what he had lost and frankly didn't care. "Bilbo could not find much pity in his heart."[26]

Then Gollum became suspicious that Bilbo had found his ring (which he had) and, with a hiss, gave chase. Bilbo rushed back up the passage and tripped, and the ring popped onto his finger—and *poof!*—he was invisible. Gollum raced past him, so the hobbit followed until Gollum had gone as close to the goblins' gate as he dared. Then he sat down and began weeping. Bilbo contemplated killing him to get past. After all, that foul thing had meant to kill *him*, hadn't it? Bilbo didn't know for sure. Then, in that instant, he grasped Gollum's condition: he had spent endless years alone in the darkness, without light or hope. He had a look into Gollum's misery, and his heart was filled with compassion. He realized he *couldn't* take his life.

Frodo later lamented that it was a pity Bilbo hadn't killed Gollum when he had the chance, but Gandalf replied, "Pity? It was Pity that stayed his hand."[27]

By pity, of course, Gandalf meant compassion. To have compassion, you must get a glimpse of where someone else is at and feel empathy for them.

Instead of despising our enemies, we must remember that they, too, are human and that God cares for them, too—as much as He hates what they're doing. We must have pity on the fallen, those who are hurting not only themselves but others—even when the "others" they're hurting are *us*. If we seek to live the gospel, we must love more than just our family and friends; we are also to love those who have evil intentions toward us, who gossip against us, and who seek to defraud us. Jesus said it like this: "Love your enemies, bless those who curse you, do good to those who hate you, and pray for those who spitefully use you and persecute you, that you may be sons of your Father in heaven" (Matthew 5:44–45 NKJV).

This doesn't mean we should *trust* our enemies—any more than Bilbo trusted Gollum. Nor does it mean we should do foolish things like open prison doors and let the criminally insane out on the streets. But we should have enough pity on our enemies—the personal ones and the ones who would do harm in society—to pray for them. We should care enough to do good to them whenever we have the opportunity. Refraining from taking revenge on an enemy and refusing to do evil to someone who hates us is already "doing good". . .and a huge step in the right direction.

Also, praying for and loving our enemies doesn't mean allowing ourselves to be their targets for attack. Like Bilbo, we must do our best to stay out of harm's way. Jesus said, "I am sending you out as sheep among wolves. So be as shrewd as snakes and harmless as doves" (Matthew 10:16 NLT). That means that if those who seek to do us ill are as cunning as snakes, we must be as shrewd as they are and stay one step ahead of them.

Yet despite everything, Jesus tells us to love our enemies. By "love" He doesn't mean we must feel the same warm, tender affection we feel for those who are dearest to us. That's probably not going to happen, but we must understand that no matter how badly someone behaves, he or she is still God's creation and, as such, still has a spark of humanity. All humans were created in the "image of God" (Genesis 1:27), and though we have all fallen—with some falling more colossally than others—we should still hold out hope that God will restore even the worst of them— just as He did us.

When we acknowledge that there is still hope for someone, then we are already demonstrating empathy for that person. And empathy moves us to compassion, and compassion moves us to acts of mercy. And when we show our enemies mercy, we're showing them God's love.

Our compassion may not seem to benefit those who

badmouth or mistreat us—or even stop them from doing such things. Our prayers may not be enough to immediately change hardened criminals for the better. But showing such people God's love will do wonders in transforming our own lives.

22

The Rings of Power

He wanted it because it was a ring of power, and if you
slipped that ring on your finger, you were invisible.
THE HOBBIT, CHAPTER 5

Gollum desired the ring because it made him invisible,
which allowed him to sneak around and do his devious deeds. Then it ended up in Mr. Baggins's possession,
and he discovered its magical properties quite by accident.
Tolkien tells us, "He had heard of such things, of course,
in old old tales."[28] Although Bilbo was surprised to have
actually come across one, he *had* known that such rings
existed.

Long ages past, the dark lord Sauron had come to the

elves pretending to be a messenger sent from the Undying Lands. He showed Celebrimbor, leader of the elvish smiths, how to create wondrous rings that enhanced their power. Of the rings Celebrimbor created under Sauron's tulelage, seven would go to the leaders of the dwarves, nine to the kings of mortal men, and three to the elves. (The elvish rings alone were unsullied by Sauron's touch.) Sauron then went off and secretly created "One Ring to rule them all"—to enslave all who wore Rings of Power.[29]

But in a great war some two thousand years later, Sauron lost the One Ring.

Now, in practice for making the nineteen Rings of Power, Celebrimbor and his smiths had created many lesser rings, "some more potent than some less."[30] Many of these rings made their way into the world at large. Bilbo assumed he now possessed one of *these* rings, when in fact it was none other than the Ruling Ring. The One Ring was filled with Sauron's malice and capable of corrupting even the noblest person. Fortunately, Bilbo wore it sparingly, so it didn't wholly corrupt him.

The parallels between Sauron and Satan can't be missed, especially since Tolkien refers to the "absolute Satanic rebellion and evil of...Sauron."[31] Just as Sauron came to the elves pretending to be a good entity while scheming to enslave them, Satan seeks to deceive and dominate people, often using things God intended for good to ensnare them: "For Satan himself transforms himself into an angel of light. Therefore it is no great thing if his ministers also transform themselves into ministers of righteousness" (2 Corinthians 11:14–15 NKJV).

Unfortunately, some believers today extend their hands to receive a Ring of Power—in the form of a doctrine or teaching that empowers them to do what they long to do, even when it's outside God's plan.

For example, sex is a gift of God and something to be desired, yet sexual immorality often ends in pain and grief, however enthralling it may seem at first. What is good and beautiful, when corrupted by the enemy, brings people into bondage. Yet those who desire license to fulfill their lusts often tune in to worldviews teaching that they're free to live however they choose. This is nothing new; the apostles repeatedly repudiated such licentious doctrines (see 1 Corinthians 5:1–3; 6:13–18; 2 Peter 2:12–22).

Some Christians, on the other hand, embrace prosperity teachings, which tell them that God's primary delight is to give them the desires of their hearts—even when their hearts covet materialistic "blessings" and financial abundance above everything else. This kind of doctrine leads them to ignore the Bible's warning that covetousness is equal to idolatry (Colossians 3:5). In the right hands, money can be used to do great good. But a selfish desire for wealth is as corrupting as wearing Sauron's ring, because "those who desire to be rich fall into temptation and a snare, and into many foolish and harmful lusts" (1 Timothy 6:9 NKJV).

Likewise, believers can use power and influence to accomplish good things. Too often, though, a person with power and influence may use them for noble purposes at first, only to use them later to manipulate and control others. (That's why Gandalf refused the One Ring when Frodo offered it to him.) When we desire undue power, it's usually so we can impose our will upon other people and get them to do what we want them to do. When this takes place in the political arena, it's called dictatorship, but when it shows up in Christian circles, it's known as legalism—and it brings people under bondage to rules and regulations.

Such teachings may seem good and desirable in the beginning—and they may even appear to be of some benefit. But an inordinate focus on rules and regulations will inevitably ensnare, corrupt, and bring into bondage those who embrace them. This is what the Bible means when it says, "While they promise them liberty, they themselves are slaves of corruption; for by whom a person is overcome, by him also he is brought into bondage" (2 Peter 2:19 NKJV).

Be wary. Satan seeks to deceive and ensnare people today through every means at his disposal. Some of them are obviously malignant things like illegal drugs, ill-gotten wealth, and illicit sex, but we can also come under the power of "good" things. So beware the Rings of Power in *whatever* form they seek to enter your life.

23

A Nearly Derailed Miracle

He tried to squeeze through the crack.
He squeezed and squeezed, and he stuck!
It was awful. . .he could not get through.
THE HOBBIT, CHAPTER 5

After leaping over Gollum, Bilbo dashed down the final passage and raced toward the Back Door and freedom. Suddenly, he rounded a corner and burst into an open space—the goblins' guard room. On the far side of the room was an open stone door, but the chamber was literally swarming with orcs.

At that moment, the ring slipped off Bilbo's finger, and he became visible. The orcs roared with delight and charged. Instantly, the hobbit thrust his finger back into the ring and vanished again. The orcs ran around wildly looking for him, so Bilbo ducked behind a barrel to avoid being trampled. Meanwhile, a guard pushed the gate nearly shut, and Bilbo realized he *had* to get to the door before they decided to close it all the way.

Finally the invisible Mr. Baggins made a run for it. He dodged this way and that, avoiding goblins, and at last reached the door. But his large brass buttons caught on the door's edge, and he was stuck. Just then, an orc saw the hobbit's shadow and sounded the alarm. Bilbo strained with all his might and, with one final effort, pushed through. The buttons exploded off his coat, but he was free!

Think of it: after being trapped over two days in the orcs' subterranean dwellings, Bilbo had been guided to the very gate that led to freedom. Not only that, but he was now invisible. It seemed that he'd be able to creep silently right past the guards. But at that point, two glitches happened. First, the ring slipped off his finger, exposing him to danger. Second, someone nearly shut the door. Murphy hadn't even been born yet, but his law was already in effect—whatever *could* go wrong *was* going wrong.

As his escape plan began to unravel, only Bilbo's quick thinking and determined action saved the day.

Like they did with Mr. Baggins, it often seems as

though our miracles have a way of running out of steam at the most critical time. We pray and pray and wait and wait, and finally—to our immense relief—at the eleventh hour, our miracle comes rolling into the station. . .only to nearly go off the rails at 11:30. We get an extension of time to finish a project, but then our computer crashes and we're scrambling to salvage the work. Desperately needed, much-prayed-for finances come through at the last minute, but then a banking hitch brings everything to a grinding halt.

Why does this happen? Why does God so often allow solutions to our problems to discombobulate at the last minute?

One reason may be that He wants to see how badly we want the answer. We pray for God to answer our prayers, but are we also willing to fight for them to make them a reality? God sends the solutions our way, yes, but sometimes He expects us to then grab hold of them and make them work. True, sometimes when God does a miracle, He does the whole thing. He basically says, "Just stand back and watch Me take care of the situation" (see Exodus 14:14; 2 Chronicles 20:17). But the Bible says that God often *helped* His people win a battle or deal with an emergency (Psalm 118:13).

These crises are not always God's doing, however. After

all, Satan constantly fights God's will tooth and nail. That's often why we have to pray so much and wait so long for answers to prayer. For example, the prophet Daniel once prayed for twenty-one days before God sent an angel with the answer. When the angel finally arrived, he told Daniel his prayers had been heard from the first day he'd prayed them but that a demon prince had fought all that time to prevent him from getting through (Daniel 10:1–13).

The devil and his demons constantly try to hinder God's purposes. The apostle Paul told the Christians of Thessalonica, "We wanted to come to you—even I, Paul, time and again—but Satan hindered us" (1 Thessalonians 2:18 NKJV). Yes, Satan tries to stop God's will by creating obstacles and delays every step of the way. Sometimes, as in Daniel's and Paul's cases, the devil works to delay answers to prayer, even though he can't stop them completely.

Often when we see our miracle coming into the station, we stop praying and start jumping for joy or slumping in relief. . .but we shouldn't be caught off guard if the devil throws a final wrench into the machinery to try to sabotage our victory. That's why we need to fight for our answer until the end. If our miracle starts to stall when it's just about to cross the finish line, we need to grab hold of it and help push it the last few steps.

And yes, apart from giving it our best effort, we need to keep on praying. As Jesus said, we "should always pray and not give up" (Luke 18:1 NIV).

24

Counting Your Blessings

After all they had lost a good deal, but. . .they had all escaped,
so they might be said to have had the best of it so far.
THE HOBBIT, CHAPTER 6

After escaping the goblins, Bilbo hurried out of a high valley and scurried down the mountainside. Then he began wondering whether or not Gandalf and the dwarves had made it out. He had just resolved to go back to find them. . .when he heard voices. It was Thorin and company! Tolkien doesn't tell us how they had escaped, but since Gandalf *knew* about the Back Door and had repeatedly fought orcs in his race toward it, it's not rocket science to figure out that they'd battled their way out the same gate from which Bilbo had just emerged.

They were mighty happy to see the hobbit again and insisted he tell them how he'd escaped. Bilbo told them the entire story. . .*except* the part about the magic ring. (For the time being, he told himself, that'd be his little secret.)

Although they were free, they had lost their ponies and all their baggage, weapons, tools, musical instruments, spare clothing, and food. In addition, Bilbo had lost most of his beautiful brass buttons and had torn his clothing. (This may seem a petty loss, but appearances *were* important to the hobbit.) Nevertheless, they realized they were doing well to be alive and free, not locked up in snake pits. They also noted that they'd gained a rather impressive victory by killing the Great Goblin.

All this was true, but Gandalf reminded them that they needed to keep moving. That's when Bilbo realized he hadn't eaten in three days; and now that the adrenaline had worn off, he was so hungry that he felt physically weak.

When we endure severe setbacks or suffer loss, and the magnitude of what we've lost threatens to overwhelm us, counting our blessings can help give us a brighter perspective. Like Bilbo and the dwarves did, we must see the upside of the situation. Instead of moaning, "My life is ruined!" we should run through a list of what we still have. Counting our blessings may seem like a childish mental exercise to cheer ourselves up, but it's a lot more than that. Sometimes it's all that gives us hope to go on after a personal disaster, like when a flood or fire has wreaked havoc in our home or we've lost valuable possessions in a break and entry.

On a later occasion, after Mr. Baggins had freed Thorin from prison using less-than-ideal methods, the dwarf complained about what he'd endured. "Well, are you alive or are you dead?" Bilbo asked him. "Are you still in prison, or are you free?"[32]

At times, those are the kind of questions we need to ask ourselves.

The reality is that life is more difficult after we've suffered loss. Not only have we lost objects that held deep emotional value, but we may also have lost a lot of practical, helpful things we use every day. As a result, we may also have to endure physical and financial hardships for some time. In addition, the crisis that dealt us a body blow may not be fully over. These can be very discouraging developments with the potential to take the wind out of our sails— and that's why we need to focus on as many encouraging thoughts as we can.

In addition, as Christians, we can pray to God for the strength to carry on, and "God, who comforts the downcast," will comfort and send help to us (2 Corinthians 7:6 NIV).

We also keep a positive attitude by staying focused on

Jesus. The Bible says it like this: "And let us run with endurance the race God has set before us. We do this by keeping our eyes on Jesus, the champion who initiates and perfects our faith. Because of the joy awaiting him, he endured the cross, disregarding its shame. . . . Think of all the hostility he endured from sinful people; then you won't become weary and give up" (Hebrews 12:1–3 NLT).

A third way to stay positive is to remember that our *eternal* wealth is in heaven, not here on earth. Jesus said, "Do not lay up for yourselves treasures on earth, where moth and rust destroy and where thieves break in and steal; but lay up for yourselves treasures in heaven, where neither moth nor rust destroys and where thieves do not break in and steal" (Matthew 6:19–20 NKJV).

We still suffer emotionally and physically when we lose belongings—there's no getting around that. But if we place a higher value on eternal treasures and rewards than on physical possessions—and if we know that no matter what happens down here, the rewards are waiting for us in eternity—it helps take some of the sting out of our loss.

That encourages us, and we *need* to be encouraged. After all, until the day we receive our eternal rewards, we still have lives to live here on earth. There's still a long road ahead.

25

Being a Decent Fellow

"I can't be always carrying burglars on my back," said Dori, "down tunnels and up trees! What do you think I am? A porter?"
THE HOBBIT, CHAPTER 6

When Gandalf had led Thorin and company from the goblins' central cave, they were all chained together with Bilbo in the very back, behind the dwarf Dori. Since barefoot Bilbo couldn't run as fast as the dwarves with their thick boots in the rough, dark tunnel, Dori had let the hobbit climb up on his shoulders. After Gandalf cut their chains, the dwarves took turns carrying Bilbo, but eventually good ol' Dori ended up carrying him again.

Now that they'd escaped the orcs, they made their way down the forested mountain flank to a clearing. Suddenly they heard a wolf's cry—then more and more wolves began howling around them. (These evil wolves of The Wild were called wargs, and they were allies of the goblins.) Gandalf urged everyone to quickly climb trees, and the dwarves, being slightly taller than Bilbo, jumped up, grabbed the lower branches, and scrambled to safety. That's when they saw the hobbit running around below, unable to get up into a tree.

When Nori accused Dori of leaving Bilbo behind, Dori complained that he wasn't a bag boy. But Bilbo was about to be devoured, so since Dori *was* closest to the ground, he climbed down to the lowest branch and stretched out his hand. Bilbo still couldn't reach it, so he descended to the ground and let Bilbo stand on his back and jump up into the tree. At that moment, hundreds of wargs loped into the clearing. Dori leaped up, grabbed a branch and swung out of reach. . .just as a warg snapped its jaws after him.

Bilbo later wrote, "Dori was really a decent fellow in spite of his grumbling."[33] Indeed he was! He'd risked his *life* to rescue Mr. Baggins.

Do we have the responsibility to carry others on our backs, the way Dori repeatedly carried Bilbo, or is it each man for his own? Don't we all have the responsibility to carry our own weight? Yes, we all have to make our own way through life. No one should shirk his or her own duties and expect others to pick up the slack. Yet we *do* have the responsibility to reach out and help the less fortunate and the disadvantaged among us. And we are certainly to help those who desperately need it. Yes, we *are* our "brother's keeper" (Genesis 4:9), and yes, God expects us to look out for others just as we look out for ourselves.

Jesus said the greatest commandment was to love God with all of our hearts and the second greatest commandment was to love our neighbor as much as we love ourselves. When someone asked, "And who exactly is my neighbor?" Jesus told the story of a man from Samaria. The Samaritans and Jews despised one another in those days, yet when robbers attacked a Jew traveling the Jericho road and left him for dead, none of his fellow countrymen stopped to help him. Only a Samaritan had enough compassion to stop and help. He cleaned his wounds, set him on his own donkey, and took him to an inn, where he paid the innkeeper to continue to care for him (Luke 10:25–37).

Jesus pointed out that the Samaritan who went out of his way to help this Jewish man was the one who obeyed God's command to love his neighbor—he was the one being "a decent fellow."

God doesn't expect us to do for others what they can do for themselves, but He's made it clear throughout the

Bible—in both the Old Testament and New Testament—that we have a responsibility to take thought of the weak and physically challenged members in our society. We are especially to help the one who is in dire straits—even if that person happens to *despise* us. Moses wrote, "If you see the donkey of someone who hates you fallen down under its load, do not leave it there; be sure you help them with it" (Exodus 23:5 NIV).

Yes, you read that right. The Bible actually *does* say that.

There are oodles of different ways you can apply this principle today—so even if your neighbor doesn't own a donkey, you're not off the hook. How about the mumbling, grumbling neighbor who's always asking you to do things for him or her—and who never seems to be properly thankful after you do them? It's enough to leave you feeling a little grumbly yourself!

Sometimes we might grumble a little when we feel like *we* always seem to be asked to help. We may not even particularly *feel* like doing a charitable deed, but acts of genuine love are not always accompanied by warm feelings of affection or attachment. When we make a conscious decision to obey God by showing love to others, the feelings very often follow.

When someone is in need, we shouldn't wait until we *feel* in a helpful mood to reach out.

26

Stepping into Your Dream

In spite of the dangers of this far land bold men had of late
been making their way back into it from the South.
THE HOBBIT, CHAPTER 6

In olden times, men had lived in these distant reaches of Wilderland. They had dwelled in the valley of the Anduin River—between the Misty Mountains in the west and Mirkwood Forest in the east, between the Carrock on the north and the Gladden River in the south.[34] Some of them had eventually migrated to the plains in the south and become the Riders of Rohan. Others had been pushed south later—probably by orcs—and had lived *near* Rohan for many years.

Now they were returning north to reclaim their home-land—*this* in spite of the fact that Sauron was in Dol Gul-dur, not far to the southeast, and his shadow had fallen over most of Mirkwood. Worse yet, in recent years orcs had been spreading throughout the Misty Mountains on the west. And the north was "simply stiff with goblins."[35]

Now wargs were about to join the orc army in a great raid against nearby settlements of men. They didn't dare attack them by day because there were many courageous and well-armed woodsmen. Therefore, they'd decided to attack when they were asleep. Tolkien doesn't tell us whether or not—after Thorin and company escaped—the goblins and wargs proceeded with their raid. Later, however, Beorn warned that *if* the orcs did attack, they'd sweep across all Wilderland, right to the edge of Mirkwood.[36]

Did the woodsman survive the onslaught, if it took place? Yes. They later united with Beorn as their chief, and seventy-seven years later, the Beornings were valiant men who guarded the river ford and kept the High Pass through the Misty Mountains open.[37] The woodsmen started out by gaining a toehold in the valleys and ended up ruling the entire land, including the high passes on the far western edge of their territory.

Way to go, woodsmen!

In the Bible, God told the Israelites to go in and conquer

the land of Canaan. Their ancestors, Abraham and Isaac, had had a desert kingdom in the Negev (southern Canaan) for three hundred-some years. Jacob and his sons owned land in central Canaan—and God had promised their descendants the *entire* land. It was their heritage, their homeland. They just had to summon the courage to go in and claim it—*all* of it, from the valleys to the mountains. They got off to a terrific start under their leader Joshua, but even by the time he was old, the job wasn't finished. There was still plenty of land to be conquered. And although many of the tribes had settled into their inheritance, several other tribes were crowded together up in the hills, not daring to go down into the valleys and claim what God had promised them. Joshua challenged the Israelites, "How long are you going to wait before taking possession of the remaining land the LORD. . .has given to you?" (Joshua 18:3 NLT).

That's a question that could be asked of many of us today: If God has given you a dream, if He's made promises to you, how long are you going to wait before you have the faith to go in and possess what He's given you?

You gain victories by determining to step into what's rightfully yours and having the courage to claim it. You become valiant when, like the woodsmen, you put feet to your courage and head out. And, very importantly, you get the job done by not continually putting it off. When Alexander the Great was asked how he had conquered so much of the world, he answered, "By not delaying."

Perhaps God has put a dream in your heart. You feel He has called you to do something special with your life, but there are many obstacles in the way, and you know you will have to endure real hardships before your dream becomes a reality. And so you put it off month after month and year after year. You mean to get to it *some*day, but setting out on such a quest seems daunting and the possibility of failure seems high—and you want to tame as many risks and dangers as possible *before* you set out.

Sometimes it's wise to be cautious and prudent to carefully lay out your plans before making a major move. Even the woodsmen made sure they were well armed and in sufficient numbers before heading north to reclaim their homelands. So yes, you must plan carefully, do the needed risk analyses, and make the necessary preparations. But at some point, your plans and preparations will be done, and then it will be time to head out "in spite of the dangers."

Are you ready to head out and claim your dream?

27

Snatched Away by Eagles

Just at that moment the Lord of Eagles swept down
from above, seized him in his talons, and was gone.
THE HOBBIT, CHAPTER 6

Although the wolves kept Gandalf, Bilbo, and the dwarves treed, the wizard began to fight back by lighting pine cones with magical fire and hurling them down at the beasts, setting both them and the underbrush alight. Then, in the middle of the ruckus, the orcs arrived. They were delighted to see their enemies trapped and began piling brushwood and ferns under the trees they were in. They then stamped out all the fires except for those closest to the trees.

Soon the flames were burning right under the fir trees, and Bilbo could feel the heat and began choking on the smoke. Then the lower branches were ablaze. Thorin and company were in a desperate situation. That's when the goblins began laughing and mocking, "Fly away little birds! Fly away if you can!"[38] Gandalf considered a last desperate act—throwing himself down from his treetop and slaying as many enemies as he could with a final spectacular burst of magic. But just before he leaped. . .a majestic, enormous Eagle swooped down, snatched him from his perch, and winged away. The orcs howled in surprise, and the wargs went wild with anger, but more Eagles swept down from the darkened heavens and plucked Thorin and company one by one from the treetops and carried them away. The great Eagles, Tolkien tells us, were enemies of the goblins, and from their high crags had seen the commotion far below and came to investigate.

You can't help but be struck by the parallel between this scene and Jesus' description of His return to snatch away believers:

> *"For as the lightning comes from the east and flashes to the west, so also will the coming of the Son of Man be. For wherever the carcass is, there the eagles will be gathered together. Immediately after the tribulation*

of those days. . .all the tribes of the earth will mourn,
and they will see the Son of Man coming on the clouds
of heaven with power and great glory. And He will
send His angels with a great sound of a trumpet,
and they will gather together His elect from the four
winds, from one end of heaven to the other."
MATTHEW 24:27–31 NKJV

Jesus promised that during the time of the last, greatest tribulation (trouble) on Earth, when the forces of darkness seemed to be winning and there was no hope left in sight for believers, He would send His angels—like eagles—to snatch us from the midst of great persecution and carry us away to heaven.

God doesn't promise to rescue us just at the *end* of time, either. He promises to rescue us from the troubles we face during this life as well. "The righteous person faces many troubles, but the LORD comes to the rescue each time" (Psalm 34:19 NLT).

Often it seems like God waits until the last possible moment to rescue us. Wolves may be circling close around us, and we may feel the flames approaching and smell the smoke. All the while, we may have to endure the taunts and mockery of our enemies.

And then God sends His angels to rescue us.

God doesn't *always* pluck us out of our troubles, however. Sometimes He gives us the strength to stay where we are and endure the almost unendurable. In times like those, His deliverance is not a sudden, breathtaking event—like an eagle swooping down and plucking us from the midst of our temptations and trials. But God delivers us all the same.

When Daniel's three friends were thrown into the fiery furnace, they were miraculously spared and came out without even the smell of smoke on them (Daniel 3). And instead of plucking Daniel *out* of the lions' den, God sent His angels down *into* that dark, terrifying pit to shut the lions' mouths (Daniel 6:16–22).

But still other times, God's people are *not* spared. Many Christians *have* burned at the stake for their faith. They were not delivered but were allowed to go down in defeat. . .at least from their enemies' perspective. But God has promised them ultimate victory at the Resurrection, when they will be raised up to everlasting glory.

Nearly eighty years after being rescued from the burning fir tree, Gandalf faced a Balrog—a great demon of shadow and fire—in the Mines of Moria. He withstood it alone, allowing his companions to escape. . .and lost his life in the process. But Eru Ilúvatar, the Father of All, the supreme Authority, brought him back to life in even greater power and splendor than before.[39] Gandalf's fall and defeat was, in the end, not a defeat after all.

So shall it be in that day when the righteous are resurrected.

The Rapture—and the Resurrection that will take place in that same instant—will be God's ultimate rescue of His children.

28

A Fierce and Flawed Friend

He can be appalling when he is angry, though he is kind
enough if humoured. Still I warn you he gets angry easily.
THE HOBBIT, CHAPTER 7

The Eagles carried Thorin and company from the burning trees, and the next day they bore them as far as the Great River. They were safe, but without food or supplies. Now, there *was* someone nearby who could help them, but Gandalf warned everyone not to annoy him, for he was extremely powerful and had a quick temper.

His name was Beorn, which means "bear" and "great warrior" in Old English, and he was a giant of a man. Beorn had a thick black beard and hair and wore a wool

145

tunic that left his powerfully muscled arms and lower legs exposed. He was formidable enough in human form, but more so when he morphed into a gigantic black bear.

Beorn had a special hatred for orcs. He belonged to a race of man-bears that had lived in the Misty Mountains, but goblins had slain all of them except for Beorn himself. He had moved east of the Anduin River, where he built a great log house, dwelled with tame horses, cattle, dogs, and sheep, and raised bees. Although Beorn was kind to animals (like a grizzly bear version of St. Francis), he had such a fierce reputation that goblins dared not come within a hundred miles of his house. He stuck a goblin's head on a stake in his yard to underscore that they weren't welcome.

Gandalf avoided angering Beorn by introducing Bilbo and the dwarves slowly (two at a time), while telling him about their adventures. When Beorn was convinced they were foes of the orcs, he kindly helped them with all the food and supplies they needed for the next leg of their journey.

He was one of the good guys after all.

The pages of the Bible are full of stories about rough "good guys"—though you sometimes wonder if they can even be called that. God chose King Saul, and he courageously led the Israelites in battle after battle against their oppressors on all sides. Yet he had a violent temper and was plagued by fits of jealousy (1 Samuel 14:47–48; 18:8–11). Joab was David's most loyal general, but he was so ruthless that David could barely stand him (2 Samuel 3:20–34). King Jehu was mightily effective in ridding Israel of Baal worship—yet he did so in a manner more violent than was necessary (2 Kings 9–10).

God has a purpose even for such flawed heroes, though that is hardly an excuse for those who are quick to blow their tops. The Bible, after all, tells us, "Control your temper, for anger labels you a fool" (Ecclesiastes 7:9 NLT).

Many people are angry for very unfortunate reasons. Beorn, for example, had been deeply wounded in his past. It helps you understand another person's anger a little better when you understand the roots of their anger. Of course, those with a temper still have an obligation to understand their issues, to seek out help, and to learn to control their anger.

Now, it's one thing to be polite and patient with a total stranger with an anger problem. Most of us can manage that. It's quite another matter to live with—or share a workplace with—someone who gets angry easily or who makes us feel like we need to walk on eggshells to avoid upsetting him or her. Nevertheless, we can't always choose our family members, relatives, or workmates. So we must find a way of dealing with them *while* they're dealing with their issues.

Gandalf's gentleness, humor, and wisdom helped bring out Beorn's best side and serves as a good example of how to do that.

Some of us (who have rather Beorn-like tendencies ourselves) have little patience with difficult people and little inclination to deal with them gently. If we'd been Gandalf, we'd have bluntly demanded that Beorn help, and when he refused, we'd have told him off. When he became furious, we'd have felled him with a wizardly lightning bolt, *taken* food and supplies, and stomped off indignantly.

Some solution! Had Gandalf approached the matter this way, Thorin and company wouldn't have received Beorn's urgent warning that the goblins were pursuing them. And in the Battle of Five Armies some months later—when the combined forces of men, elves, and dwarves were about to be overrun—Beorn would *not* have shown up full of great wrath against the orcs and saved the day.

There's wisdom in the madness of dealing gently with angry people—especially when you know that beneath their gruff exterior and temper they have a kind heart and generous disposition.

And hey, there's hope that they *will* change. Beorn did!

29

Waiting till It's Time

"I have, as I told you, some pressing business away south;
and I am already late through bothering with you people."
THE HOBBIT, CHAPTER 7

Although Gandalf had traveled with Thorin and company to the very edge of Mirkwood, he had made it clear he wouldn't be accompanying them all the way to Lonely Mountain. Now Gandalf told them he could accompany them no longer. He was, in fact, late for a meeting of the White Council, which was gathering to decide what to do about the Necromancer in Dol Guldur.

When Tolkien wrote *The Hobbit*, he arranged Gandalf's departure so that Bilbo and the dwarves would face the rest of their adventure alone. But when he was writing *The Lord of the Rings*, Tolkien realized that Gandalf's mission in the south of Mirkwood was even more important than the dwarves' quest. The Necromancer was the dark lord Sauron, who was even now rebuilding armies of orcs to overrun Middle-earth.

Tolkien gives us no further details about this in *The Hobbit*, but we learn from other writings that although Gandalf was concerned about the injustice done to the dwarves, his primary concern was not to help them retake their gold and their kingdom—that was only incidental in the grand scheme. First and foremost in Gandalf's mind was the fact that Sauron might enlist the help of the dragon to devastate northern Middle-earth.[40] The fact that the dwarves would have to somehow *kill* the dragon in order to regain their gold was what convinced Gandalf to help them.

So often, we're wrapped up in our own needs and pray almost exclusively for God to help us fulfill our own dreams and desires. Like Thorin, we brood over our personal losses and plot and plan down through the years so we can regain them. After all, we figure, God *is* a God of justice, and He wants us to have what is rightfully ours. But as Solomon said, "To everything there is a season, a time for every purpose under heaven" (Ecclesiastes 3:1 NKJV).

If you do the math, you'll see that Thorin had to wait 171 years after Smaug's attack before his purposes (revenge on Smaug and regaining his gold) lined up with the larger purposes.[41]

Even for a long-lived dwarf, 171 years is a long time to wait. . .and wait. . .and wait. . . .

The Bible tells us to pray but doesn't promise that we can always expect answers immediately. We're told to *keep* on praying and not give up asking. Jesus illustrated this truth when He told a parable about a judge who kept putting off dealing with an injustice a poor widow had suffered. The woman kept coming to him with her case, over and over again, until finally he realized that she simply wasn't going to give up. . .and then he helped her. Of course, God isn't reluctant to help us, but He often requires us to wait.

Jesus summed up this parable by saying, "Shall God not avenge His own elect who cry out day and night to Him, though He bears long with them? I tell you that He will avenge them speedily" (Luke 18:7–8 NKJV). In this context, to "avenge" does not necessarily mean to do violence to anyone but instead to bring justice, to set things right.

But perhaps you're thinking, *I don't need God to avenge me—not on Smaug, not on anyone else—but I do desperately need Him to answer my prayers.* Well, the same principle applies. You must trust that God is going to answer your prayers, and you must have the patience to wait until He does.

Jesus' brother James wrote, "See how the farmer waits for the land to yield its valuable crop, patiently waiting for the autumn and spring rains" (James 5:7 NIV). No matter how soon they *wanted* the harvest to take place, the Israelites couldn't even begin to *plant* until the autumn rains had softened the hard, parched soil. And they couldn't *harvest* before the spring rains came, because the heads of grain hadn't ripened yet. It took those final rains to fully mature the barley and wheat, and the rains happened in their proper season. . .and not before. So the farmers waited patiently.

When the time is right, God *will* answer prayer. Until then, we need to pray, to have patience, and to not give up.

Of course, not only do we have to wait for God's time, we have to make sure what we're asking for is in His will. All situations are different, so we can't simply assume that our specific prayers will be answered if we "have enough faith," or if we nag God persistently enough. The apostle Paul learned that lesson after he prayed repeatedly for God to heal his physical disability. Paul called it his "thorn in the flesh," and from the way he described it, it sounds like an eye disease. In this case, God *didn't* heal him but instead gave him the grace to live with it (2 Corinthians 12:7–9). But if what you're asking for *is* God's will, you can pray confidently (1 John 5:14–15).

30

Forgetting the Forest

It was not long before they grew to hate the forest. . . .
But they had to go on and on, long after they were
sick for a sight of the sun and of the sky.
THE HOBBIT, CHAPTER 8

Beorn had given Thorin and company enough food to last them a couple weeks while they followed the path through Mirkwood and had also loaned them ponies to ride to the forest's edge. Now they sent the ponies back to Beorn, hoisted the heavy packs of food on their backs, and plunged reluctantly into the deep, dark woods. The path was narrow, and the depths it wound through were dismal and gloomy even by day, and pitch black at night.

After sunset, the darkness came alive with bright eyes looking out at them. But whatever the creatures were, they didn't attack. . .not yet. Instead, a different, more insidious danger closed in on them—sheer, hypnotic tedium.

Day after day, they trudged in and out among the trees. It was like walking on an endless treadmill in the sunless gloom, and soon monotony set in, numbing their minds and senses. They pushed dispiritedly through dimness, longing for a glimpse of sun and sky. It wasn't long before they *hated* the forest. When Bilbo was lost in the goblins' tunnels, fear had sapped his strength, for danger had been all around. Here, though, boredom leeched away his spirit.

Unless you've been lost in the sameness of a northern boreal forest, with identical pine trees for hundreds of miles in every direction, you may not grasp how the dwarves felt in the murky depths of Mirkwood. Or if you've worked the midnight shift in a sunless factory at a job you hated, month after month, you just might understand.

Sometimes we're forced to take on jobs we don't particularly like simply because we need to pay the bills. The wages may be good, or they may be mediocre, but if we constantly feel unchallenged and unfulfilled, we can begin to hate that job. God sometimes calls us to tasks where there's a measure of danger or financial insecurity, and it takes faith and courage to stick to the path. Other times, however, He calls us to jobs that provide much more financial security but little to challenge us—leaving us bored out of our skulls, feeling like we're dying, and crying out for change.

At such times, it takes strong resolve (and a positive attitude) to stay the course.

Also, even very boring jobs eventually come to an end. According to Tolkien, it took Thorin and company seven days to reach the Enchanted Stream in the *middle* of Mirkwood—meaning it would have taken them only two weeks to cross the entire forest.

Gandalf's advice to the dwarves before they entered the gloomy woods was, "Think of the treasure at the end, and forget the forest."[42] The Bible gives similar advice: "Therefore do not cast away your confidence, which has great reward. For you have need of endurance, so that after you have done the will of God, you may receive the promise" (Hebrews 10:35–36 NKJV).

Okay, so we need endurance. But how do we get it? Often the simplest and best way is to "forget the forest" around us and keep our eyes on our future hope, not on the present weary, dreary reality of the daily routine.

This is not the same as "working for the weekend"—though weekends can be welcome breaks. This means we need to keep our eyes on the treasure at the end of life's journey, not just the leisure at the end of the week. We won't make it if we try to drag ourselves through our job, hating each step of the way. Eventually, zombie workers get laid off or stumble brain-dead into a workplace accident. Either that or they walk out the door and join the long lines of the unemployed.

And this isn't just true in the workplace, either. If we become bored in our walk with the Lord—if we go through the motions of living the Christian life (attend church merely out of habit and find no interest in prayer or Bible reading)—we face a danger of becoming the living dead in the spiritual sense. Jesus told a church going through this kind of malaise in New Testament times, "I know your works, that you have a name that you are alive, but you are dead" (Revelation 3:1 NKJV).

Life is sometimes very exciting—almost *too* nail-bitingly exciting. But other times it can be so maddeningly calm—with one day very much like another—that it all becomes routine and boring. That's when we need perseverance and endurance. Instead of simply giving up and sitting down by the side of the forest path, we need to gain our second wind and keep on going. We do that by keeping our eyes on the finish line, where a great reward is waiting for us.

Although we can't always change our circumstances, we *can* change our attitudes.

31

Overcoming a Deep Fear

At the best of times heights made Bilbo giddy...
and he had never liked ladders, let alone trees.
THE HOBBIT, CHAPTER 6

After trudging through the woods for many, many days, Bilbo and the dwarves were almost out of food, so Thorin decided somebody had to climb a tree to see how close they were to the forest's edge. The dwarves were too heavy to climb into the thin, uppermost branches, so it had to be Bilbo—the hobbit was the only one light enough.

To make the climb, however, Mr. Baggins had to overcome some of his fears. In addition to suffering from astraphobia (fear of lightning), Bilbo also had a classic case of acrophobia (fear of heights). This was common in the Shire. In fact, Tolkien tells us, "Hobbits do not like heights, and do not sleep upstairs, even when they have any stairs."[43] That's why all the rooms in Bilbo's hobbit hole were on the same floor. As for trees, most hobbits considered climbing them to be as crazy as crossing an unknown ocean.

Fear of heights is no joke. If a person with acrophobia attempted to climb a ladder or a tree, he would likely begin to shake, sweat, and have heart palpitations. He may even become paralyzed with fear and have difficulty thinking.

But Bilbo actually managed to climb the tree without suffering a numbing paralysis. The only problem was that when he reached the uppermost branches, he could see nothing but forest in every direction.

What changed Mr. Baggins? How did he overcome this phobia?

Well, he had scrambled to the top of fir tree a few weeks earlier to escape hundreds of wolves. His lupophobia (fear of wolves) was considerably stronger than his acrophobia, and it had driven the lesser fear from his mind. Then, an eagle carried him for some time at dizzying heights. These combined experiences seemed to have given him a considerable measure of victory over his phobia of heights. After that, climbing a ladder or tree was no big deal for him.

This is not a recommended way of overcoming phobias,

but it has been known to work. It's not generally advised that those with exaggerated worries or irrational fears continue to avoid the feared object or situation but that they gradually confront those fears and slowly build confidence. This involves not only physically facing the phobia but also dealing with it mentally—in other words, convincing oneself the fear is irrational. Some 19 million Americans suffer from some kind of phobia, and what works for one person may not work best for another—but generally this is the recommended approach.

When it comes to overcoming fear, those of us with faith in God have an additional advantage. God is interested not only in protecting us from *real* danger but also in helping us overcome *imagined* threats. God often calls upon us to face even our deepest fears. Like Bilbo, we're sometimes plunged directly into them without warning. We're given no time to warm up to the idea, to calmly and rationally decide, "Okay now, I can *do* this." Instead, we're dropped into the situation—and yes, we feel fright.

King David admitted that he felt alarmed at times, but he also stated that he had learned from experience what to do in such situations: cry out to the Lord. David once said to God, "Whenever I am afraid, I will trust in You" (Psalm 56:3 NKJV).

Notice that David didn't say, "*If* I am afraid"—as if he

were so brave that he wasn't likely to suffer apprehension. He said, "*Whenever* I am afraid." David knew fear, but he also knew how to deal with it—by trusting in God.

Trusting in God simply means you believe God will protect you. It means making a conscious effort to turn focus from your fear and onto God. This is why David also said, "Though I walk through the valley of the shadow of death, I will fear no evil; for You are with me" (Psalm 23:4 NKJV).

When you feel a numbing panic rising within you—especially when you know it's due to your particular phobia—it's good to meditate on biblical promises such as the following: "God has not given us a spirit of fear, but of power and of love and of a sound mind" (2 Timothy 1:7 NKJV). Fear causes us to be weak. It paralyzes our thinking and makes our minds *un*sound. But God isn't the one who makes us feel that way. Rather, much of the devil's power is in using our anxieties and fears against us. When he does that, all we have to do is remember that God is much more powerful than the enemy, and that He can cast the fear out of us (1 John 4:18).

Fear is a very common human emotion, and that's why the Bible has so much to say about it—and also why it tells us how to overcome it.

32

The Dark Night of the Soul

He felt like a different person, and much fiercer and bolder in spite of an empty stomach, as he wiped his sword on the grass and put it back into its sheath.
THE HOBBIT, CHAPTER 8

Bilbo was separated from the dwarves in the dark, gloomy woods. This was one of the most utterly miserable moments in his life. He eventually nodded off, but he was later startled awake to find sticky cords wrapped around his legs. He tried to get up but fell over, and instantly the giant spider that had been binding him tried to poison him. The hobbit desperately fought the creature off. As he drew his sword, the spider sprang back, giving

Mr. Baggins the opportunity he needed to cut his legs free from the cords.

Then Bilbo went on the offensive. He struck the spider in the eyes with his sword, and as it danced around in its death throes, he dispatched it with a final stroke. The horrid monster fell down dead—and Bilbo fainted. When he came to the next morning, he saw the spider lying lifeless and his sword on the ground, its blade stained black with arachnid blood. Bilbo had done the unimaginable: by himself with no one to help, he faced a nightmare creature in pitch blackness, and he had slain it.

It would be an understatement to say Bilbo's confidence level had risen. He was a changed hobbit.

This was not a stand-alone event in Bilbo's life. Rather, it was the culmination of a long series of events that had slowly, steadily toughened up, even transformed, the gentle, comfort-loving hobbit. Bilbo had endured nearly three months of privations and hunger, of imprisonment and escapes; he had been forced to face his deepest fears; he had been thrust from one danger to another. This spider crisis was the final tipping point, the moment in which the re-made Mr. Baggins rose to the occasion.

There's an old saying, "What doesn't kill you makes you stronger." But that's *not* always true. Like many other clichés, this one is often applied as a haphazard Band-aid to deep hurts. The truth is that sometimes what doesn't kill you leaves you wounded or weak. Nevertheless, it *is* true that enduring prolonged adversity generally *does* toughen you and make you stronger, whether or not you realize it. You may not *feel* stronger. Long months or years of adversity may leave you feeling worn down. You may feel weak and lost and afraid...as Bilbo did.

Yes, you can *feel* weak yet strong at the same time. The apostle Paul pointed out this paradoxical truth when he wrote, "For when I am weak, then I am strong" (2 Corinthians 12:10 NKJV).

The biblical patriarch Jacob could certainly identify with those feelings. He was forced out of the comforts of home and into a strange country, where he was toughened up by long years of adversity. Jacob said, "The heat consumed me in the daytime and the cold at night, and sleep fled from my eyes. It was like this for the twenty years I was in your household. I worked for you...and you changed my wages ten times" (Genesis 31:40–41 NIV).

Jacob was robbed, defrauded, and pursued by Laban and his clan. And now he was about to face his deadliest enemy, his brother Esau, who had with him four hundred heavily armed warriors. Jacob was at wit's end...but then his transformation came. In the dark of the night, he was forced to fight a powerful being (the Angel of the Lord), who wrestled with him till daybreak (see Genesis 32:6–7; 22–30).

The unrelenting hardships Jacob had suffered, coupled with his desperation that night, gave him a fierce tenacity, and he simply would not give up. He emerged from his battle a changed man, a stronger man. This despite the fact that the struggle ended with Jacob's hip wrenched out of joint (forever after he would walk with a limp). He emerged from that dark night physically beaten and worse for the wear—but also an overcomer, a man who had struggled with God and with men, and had prevailed (Genesis 32:28).

Jacob was weaker and more handicapped than he had ever been, yet he was stronger and more equipped than ever to face the future.

God desires to transform us, but that transformation often comes after a night of fear and discouragement, of long periods of feeling utterly lost and alone, and of despair culminating in a terrific battle in the dark. Bilbo had to go through this before he was ready to rescue his companions from an entire brood of spiders the next day, and Jacob had to go through his "dark night of the soul" before he was ready to face Esau and his army the following morning.

We, too, may have more courage and strength than we know—just waiting for a final challenge to bring them out. In that day, we, too, may rise to the occasion and do feats we never imagined we could.

33

Adrenaline and Love

He darted backwards and forwards, slashing at
the spider-threads, hacking at their legs, and
stabbing their fat bodies if they came too near.
THE HOBBIT, CHAPTER 8

A part from going for leisurely walks around the Shire, the only physical activity Bilbo took part in was playing ninepins, dart-throwing, and such—though these low-action activities were more for enjoyment than for exercise. However, after he put on his invisible ring and looked for the dwarves, Bilbo found them wrapped up in spiderwebs, hanging from a branch, about to be devoured. He had to act immediately.

Bilbo picked up stones and felled two giant spiders, then began recklessly singing an insulting song to infuriate the others. Once he'd stirred them into a frothing rage, he led them off on a merry chase through the woods. When they were some distance away, very quietly—and quite invisibly—he hurried back to the dwarves. There was one spider left guarding them, and Bilbo immediately slew it. While he was cutting the dwarves free, however, the rest of the spiders returned. Hundreds of furious, hissing arachnids surrounded them and then attacked. The dwarves were so sick and stiff they could barely defend themselves. Bilbo, however, darted here and there, thrusting and stabbing with his elvish blade.

Finally, Bilbo instructed Thorin and company to break free while he led the spiders off in another direction. The dwarves did so but were still nearly overcome by spiders. Bilbo suddenly appeared beside them, and as he hacked and slashed at the enraged monsters, Thorin and company made good on their opportunity to escape.

The spiders finally gave up the chase, and the dwarves were effusive in their praise of their most remarkable hobbit hero. Their opinion of Mr. Baggins had radically changed. Small wonder, for Bilbo himself had radically changed. This fierce monster killer bore little resemblance to the refined, genteel hobbit who had quivered like a jelly on his rug three months earlier.

Maybe adrenaline can partly account for many of Bilbo's heroic actions. After all, many a parent has suddenly found exceptional strength and courage when rescuing his or her child from danger. But long before the adrenaline kicks in, you have to *love* the one who's in danger. Before you will put yourself in harm's way for another's sake, you have to consider that person worth saving. Unless you're a professional soldier or policeman whose very job description is to "serve and protect," you won't do it. Even everyday heroes who risk their lives for total strangers are moved by a deep concern—yes, we can call it *love*—for their fellow man. This love, fueled by adrenaline, spurs them into action even in the face of great danger.

The Bible has plenty to say about this kind of love. It's what motivated Jesus to lay down His life for us: "When we were still powerless, Christ died for the ungodly. Very rarely will anyone die for a righteous person, though for a good person someone might possibly dare to die. But God demonstrates his own love for us in this: While we were still sinners, Christ died for us" (Romans 5:6–8 NIV). Jesus didn't suffer and die for us simply out of a sense of duty— love motivated Him to take the whip on His back and the nails through His hands.

And the Bible calls us to follow Jesus' example: "This is

how we know what love is: Jesus Christ laid down his life for us. And we ought to lay down our lives for our brothers and sisters" (1 John 3:16 NIV).

Bilbo certainly exemplified that self-sacrificing kind of love. He could have died a dozen times over taking on all those enormous spiders.

Fortunately, as the apostle John points out in the very next verse, laying down our lives doesn't usually mean being nailed to a cross or taking a bullet for someone. Most of the time, it means being moved by love to help someone or to give to a person in need: "If anyone has material possessions and sees a brother or sister in need but has no pity on them, how can the love of God be in that person? . . . Let us not love with words or speech but with actions and in truth" (1 John 3:17–18 NIV).

Even going out of our way to help someone takes a lot of love. You'd think that taking time out of our schedule to help others would just about kill some of us. We either groan inwardly, grit our teeth, and do it, or—better yet— we undergo an inner change first and put our hearts into helping others.

God calls us to lay down our lives for others in small, helpful, practical ways every day. No adrenaline required, just love. You don't need to be a live-action hero to be someone's hero today—you just need love to motivate you as you take whatever action—big or small—that is needed.

34

The Saruman Conspiracy

It appeared that Gandalf had been to a great council of the white wizards...and that they had at last driven the Necromancer from his dark hold in the south of Mirkwood.
THE HOBBIT, CHAPTER 19

From the snatches of conversation Bilbo heard later, it seemed that Gandalf had attended a council of white wizards. Tolkien elsewhere called it the White Council and said it included wizards as well as elves like Galadriel, Elrond, and Círdan.[44]

Now, the wizard Saruman had been appointed head of the council, and therein was Gandalf's problem. Saruman was chosen because he'd done a thorough study of the lore of Sauron and knew the most about the Rings of Power. Saruman seemed like the natural choice, but what no one knew was that Saruman, in studying Sauron's dark arts deeply, had come to desire his power. He wanted power to rule Middle-earth. . .*his* way. To do that, he concluded, *he* needed to find the One Ring before Sauron did.

Years earlier, Gandalf had suspected that the Necromancer was Sauron, so he had secretly entered his fortress of Dol Guldur, where his fears were confirmed. When the White Council met next, Gandalf urged them to drive Sauron out, but Saruman overruled him, saying they should wait. He had a devious plan: As Sauron focused on the One Ring, the Ring would reveal its own location. Then he, Saruman, would snatch it up.

Saruman thwarted Gandalf's advice and continued hindering all his plans for the next seventy-one years. This allowed Sauron to grow in power and build an army of orcs. Saruman *finally* became alarmed when Sauron came dangerously close—so he thought—to discovering the Ring. That's why Saruman finally agreed when the council met *now* and Gandalf urged them to attack. The White Council attacked Dol Guldur, and Sauron fled to Mordor.

Has something like this ever happened to you? You see a problem and take your concerns to the proper authorities, but instead of agreeing with you, they tell you to calm down and not to act rashly. Only later do you learn that these same authorities were *implicit* in the situation you brought to their attention—or had a personal stake in preserving the status quo. So they deliberately frustrated your efforts—even publicly opposing you.

It sounds like the plot of some psychological thriller, but it plays out in real life surprisingly often, and at every level of society. It's often the hidden motive of the sneaky beast called *office politics*, the unspoken reason a deserving person doesn't receive a promotion or a raise—or the cronyism and discrimination that determines why a certain person's suggestions are routinely ignored. . .or never even make it to the top boss's desk.

The prophet Jeremiah found himself in a similar bind. In his day, those in charge of the land of Judah were the corrupt and power-hungry princes, priests, and prophets. God had warned Jeremiah that because of the sins of the rulers and the people, He was going to send the Babylonians to conquer them. Over a period of many years, Jeremiah repeatedly warned the people about the internal problems and the external threat. He pled with the rulers of Judah to listen, but instead of listening, they tried to shut him up. They called him a liar and did everything they could to discredit him. They even locked him up in stocks and threw him in prison.

The rulers should have been the ones to *fix* the situation. Instead, as God had told Jeremiah, "From the least to the greatest, all are greedy for gain; prophets and priests alike, all practice deceit" (Jeremiah 6:13 NIV). God spoke to Ezekiel about the same situation: "Your princes plot conspiracies just as lions stalk their prey. They devour innocent people, seizing treasures and extorting wealth" (Ezekiel 22:25 NLT).

When the ruling princes are doing the plotting and are organizing the conspiracy, there's not a lot of hope for change!

Of course, not every person who tries to frustrate your efforts is part of a conspiracy. You could simply be dealing with stubborn people who have their own reasons—which they may not *tell* you—for wanting to stay in control and keep things the way they are. And so they frustrate your efforts for change for months. . .or years.

In fact, come to think of it, *you* could be the one resisting a needed change while refusing to reveal your real reasons for preserving the status quo. Maybe you don't want change because you're comfortable with the present routine. Maybe you refuse to switch to a new technology because the learning curve seems too steep. Or perhaps you just like the level of control you have over the present situation—and who wants to admit, "That's my *real* reason, folks"?

And so you resist change for years, offering one excuse after another.

Eventually you *will* have to change or upgrade, so why waste time fighting it? If it ain't broke, don't fix it, but if it *is* broke, then *please*, by all means fix it—or allow others to fix it.

35

Adventure on Indefinite Hold

"This is the dreariest and dullest part of all this wretched, tiresome, uncomfortable adventure!"
THE HOBBIT, CHAPTER 9

Shortly after they escaped the spiders, the dwarves were surrounded by wood-elves and marched into the cavern of King Thranduil, while Bilbo followed invisibly. Thranduil demanded that they explain why they were trespassing on his land. The Elven king coveted wealth and was eager to enlarge his hoard, so the dwarves reasoned that if they told him they were headed to Lonely Mountain to reclaim their treasure, he'd demand an exorbitant ransom. So they said nothing. Thranduil, therefore, had them locked up in prison until they gave him an answer.

All told, the dwarves were imprisoned beneath the Elven king's palace for over a month and a half. For many days, Bilbo was alone, invisible, furtively darting about in the shadows, hiding in corners, and taking food when no one was looking. He wished he could get a message out to Gandalf, but *that* was impossible. Whatever rescuing was to be done, he'd have to do it. So although he had no real hope of helping the dwarves, he found out where all their dungeons were.

The dwarves were greatly encouraged. Since Bilbo had rescued them before, they expected him to find a way to free them again. The hobbit, however, could come up with no plan: "He sat and thought and thought, until his head nearly burst, but no bright idea would come."[45]

Not only was this the dreariest and dullest part of their adventure so far, but it was also the most frustrating. . .for Bilbo *and* the dwarves. Bilbo had to do something, because no one else could. Yet what *could* he do? His movements were restricted. He was like a lone chess piece moving pointlessly back and forth on a board in the final moments of a losing game. He was boxed in with no way out.

Have you ever felt this way? You become ill, and bureaucrats decide you don't qualify for sickness benefits—so you keep submitting the same paperwork again and again, trying to convince them you qualify. Or you have an accident and the insurance company tries to deny you a big chunk of what you're rightfully due. Or you apply for a student loan, and what starts off hopeful ends up looking more and more like a maze. Or you lose your job and have to wait and wait for someone to authorize your unemployment benefits. Or you're looking for a job and constantly receive the message, "Don't call us. We'll call you." And they don't call.

Your life has been put on hold until further notice, and you're hanging in limbo. At the end of the day, you feel as though all your efforts count for nothing. You begin to feel like a hamster on a treadmill—constantly running, constantly trying to make things happen but getting nowhere. It's almost as if nothing you can do has any effect on the outcome. You're like Bilbo darting around the Elven king's halls invisible, not able to accomplish anything.

The Bible describes this sense of futility this way: "Everyone goes around like a mere phantom; in vain they rush about" (Psalm 39:6 NIV).

You know that people, not God, are the ones holding things up, but surely, you tell yourself, God could change things if He wanted them to be changed. And after awhile, when He hasn't (yet), you begin to feel that *He* is the One boxing you in week after week, month after month. Like Job, you complain, "I have been allotted months of futility" (Job 7:3 NIV). You begin to feel frustrated and upset with God—even though you know that puts you in a no-win situation. And so you continue to pace your floor, pray, and weep.

It was bad enough in prison for Bilbo, but imagine being the dwarves locked up in small cells that whole time, with all of their hopes pinned on Mr. Baggins somehow managing to think of some clever way to set them free.

But he does nothing.

And yet, just as Bilbo's thoughts were constantly on the dwarves' plight, God's thoughts *are* on you during your long days of boredom and hopelessness. . .and He *does* care. He hears you when you pray. . .and pray and pray and pray. He's not ignoring you—though at times that's precisely how it feels. The psalmist put it this way: "For the Lord hears the cries of the needy; he does not despise his imprisoned people" (Psalm 69:33 NLT).

Eventually, God will either do a miracle by making the wheels move, or He will inspire you with another solution. The rain will come and end your drought.

If you feel like your life is at its "dreariest and dullest" point right now—and that it's *been* this way for some time—you may feel like giving up. Don't. It may take awhile—sometimes *quite* awhile—but God *will* help you. He hasn't given up, and neither should you. After all, He can do the impossible.

36

Good Luck or Blessing

Luck of an unusual kind was with Bilbo then.
THE HOBBIT, CHAPTER 9

B ilbo was desperately trying to figure a way to free the
dwarves and to escape from the wood-elves. Then, as
he explored the lowest caverns, he discovered that the river
flowed beneath the palace and issued out the other side.
There *was* a chance to escape—*if* he could get hold of the
cell keys and *if* they could sneak out the water gate unde-
tected. Two very big "ifs."

That's when things fell into place. It just so happened to
be the night of the elves' great autumn feast, and there was
scarcely anyone around; they were either off celebrating in

the woods or in the palace above. The invisible Mr. Baggins listened as the chief butler told the head guard that they'd soon be dropping the empty food and wine barrels into the river so they could be carried downstream to Laketown for refills. But first, the butler poured himself and the head guard great flagons of the king's own wine. The drink was so potent, however, that both elves were soon fast asleep.

What a stroke of good luck! Bilbo quickly realized that this was his and the dwarves' best chance to escape. He tiptoed quietly up to the head guard and slipped the keys from his belt then hurried down the hall to free the dwarves.

Tolkien repeatedly referred to Bilbo having good luck. In *The Lord of the Rings*, Frodo was described as enjoying the same good luck. Some readers might be tempted to think this was simply an overused plot device—reliance on happy coincidence—but what Tolkien *literally* meant was that things were working out for the hobbits in a fortuitous manner. He'd certainly have been aware of the pagan roots of *luck* and *fortune*, but I believe he infused Christian meaning into them.

There is evidence for this. When Frodo and Sam were making their weary trek across the wastes of Mordor, Sam discovered some water and suggested that he drink it first in case it was poisonous. Frodo responded, "I think we'll trust our luck together, Sam; or our blessing."[46]

Now *blessing* is something Christians can relate to!

To be blessed, you need some deity blessing you—and the great, good deity the Free Peoples of Middle-earth worshiped was the one God, Eru Ilúvatar. It was Eru who had chosen Bilbo and Frodo and who had his hand on them.

In popular thinking, those who seem to be perpetually lucky are said to lead "charmed lives." Good things continually come their way, while misfortune always passes right on by. When they drop their toast on the floor, it always lands jam-side up, and traffic lights always turn green as they arrive at the intersection. The *other* guy gets sick—not them. As the old saying goes, everything they touch turns to gold.

We Christians can slip into this kind of thinking, especially when things are going well for us. We somehow believe that to be "blessed" means to continually receive good things *and* to avoid all bad things.

Of course, we know that the primary way God blesses us is by giving us salvation and making us His sons and daughters. With this blessing also comes peace of mind, love, and other blessings: "Blessed be the God and Father of our Lord Jesus Christ, who has blessed us with every spiritual blessing in the heavenly places in Christ" (Ephesians 1:3 NKJV).

But we also need to be blessed with our "daily bread"—as well as the *monthly* bread to pay the rent and other bills. And so we zero in on Bible verses like this one: "The blessing of the Lord makes one rich, and He adds no sorrow with it" (Proverbs 10:22 NKJV). *Right on*, we think.

And so we wonder, "What must I do to be blessed?"

The Bible tells us that "blessings are on the head of the righteous" and "a faithful man will abound with blessings" (Proverbs 10:6; 28:20 NKJV). This means that in order to receive God's full blessings, we must not be guilty of evil deeds or thoughts. "He who has clean hands and a pure heart...shall receive blessing from the Lord" (Psalm 24:4–5 NKJV). In other words, if we want God to bless us, we must be faithful to obey Him and live godly lives. And, of course, we must remember to pray and *ask* God to bless us.

But even doing all these things does not guarantee that God will supply us with unceasing material abundance, or that we will be spared all hardships, dangers, and misfortune.

Bilbo was blessed, but that doesn't mean his path was easy—no more than our lives are always easy today, even though we enjoy God's blessing. Bilbo was called upon to endure great hardships, sometimes almost more than he could bear. He ended up in tight situations again and again, and he repeatedly faced danger. But because he *was* blessed, he was eventually delivered from all his troubles.

We, too, can expect God to bless us with miraculous deliverances. It just may take time.

37

Not What We Expected

*"We thought you had got some sensible notion, when
you managed to get hold of the keys. This is a mad idea!"*
THE HOBBIT, CHAPTER 9

Bilbo knew they couldn't simply sneak from the cellar into the river below, for a large, ponderously heavy water gate was in place, lowered down to the very riverbed, to prevent unauthorized people from leaving or entering. However, he knew that wooden barrels filled with apples, butter, wine, and other provisions regularly came upriver from Laketown, and when they were empty, they were dropped into the river, the water gate was raised, and the empties floated back downstream.

There were quite a number of empty barrels waiting in the cellar, and Bilbo's idea was to pack the dwarves inside them before the elves dropped them into the river, opened the water gate, and let them go. Mr. Baggins suspected the dwarves wouldn't particularly *like* his plan, and was he ever right! Dwarves didn't suffer from claustrophobia, but they were concerned about having enough air, water leaking in, and being battered about. (You know. . .the *usual* packed-inside-a-barrel concerns.)

But they could think of no better plan, so in the end, they grudgingly agreed.

The dwarves' unconventional escape from the elves' fortress is reminiscent of Saul (the apostle Paul's name before God called him to be a missionary) escaping from the city of Damascus. This religious fanatic had gone there to persecute Christians, but he had a vision of Jesus on the way and, to everyone's surprise, became a Christian himself. When Saul began to preach the gospel in Damascus, the Christians' enemies persuaded the governor to arrest him. They watched the gates day and night to prevent him from escaping, but the Christians tied ropes to a large basket, put Saul inside it, and lowered him over the city wall (see Acts 9:23–25; 2 Corinthians 11:32–33).

The dwarves' escape also reminds us of how Moses' mother placed her son in a basket and set him in the

Nile River after the Egyptians ordered the death of all the newborn Hebrew males. She placed him among the reeds near where Pharaoh's daughter came to bathe, apparently in hopes that the princess would have mercy on her child—which she did (see Exodus 2:1–6). This was a *very* risky plan; things could have gone terribly wrong in a river where hungry crocodiles lurked.

At times we, too, have to trust in seemingly mad ideas and endure less-than-desirable solutions. Sometimes we're forced into situations where we have no alternative but to take physical or financial risks. . .or endure embarrassment at being brought so low that we must try desperate means.

Perhaps you lose your job and can't find enough work to pay your bills, so you're forced to move out of your apartment and back in with your parents. Perhaps you *do* find employment, but not the high-paying position your university degree qualifies you for, and you end up flipping burgers, waitressing, or driving a taxi to make ends (almost) meet. You never could have imagined it would come to this, but it has, and the solution—though it hardly seems like a solution at all—is the only way out of your predicament.

Sometimes you simply have to do what you have to do.

Why, you ask, does God allow us to go through such trying times? Why does He permit us to be humiliated by reducing us to such means? Didn't Jesus say, "I am come that they might have life, and that they might have it more abundantly" (John 10:10 KJV)? Part of the answer may be that we have a wrong idea of what "the abundant life" really is.

God *has* promised to supply our needs, but the abundant life Jesus referred to was primarily spiritual. If this surprises you, check out the verse directly *before* this, where Jesus said, "I am the door: by me if any man enter in, he shall be saved, and shall go in and out, and find pasture" (John 10:9 KJV). Jesus was talking about salvation, and the abundant pasture He was talking about was spiritual food and life. The green stuff He promised was *not* dollar bills.

In this life, we can't expect to be so continuously blessed that we remain untouched by illnesses, financial setbacks, or other troubles. Many Christians in New Testament times endured "a great trial of affliction" and suffered "deep poverty," but that didn't stop them from living the Christian life to the fullest (2 Corinthians 8:1–4 NKJV). Hundreds of millions of spiritually rich Christians living today in Third World countries understand this concept well.

Very often, God brings spiritual riches into our lives by allowing us to go through hard times, by squeezing us through a knothole. God is, after all, primarily concerned with developing our character—not our prestige or bank accounts or even necessarily our comfort.

38

The Fortunate Misfortune

So you see Bilbo had come in the end
by the only road that was any good.
THE HOBBIT, CHAPTER 10

The current swept the bobbing barrels—thirteen of them with a dwarf inside and invisible Bilbo riding another like it was a pony—eastward downriver. Eventually, the current carried them into a bay on the river's north shore. There, waiting elves snagged the barrels and roped them together.

The next morning, the elves climbed aboard the barrel-raft and pushed off toward Laketown. As Mr. Baggins, still invisible, traveled with them, he listened to their conversations. That's when he learned how fortunate his recent misadventures had been. Before Thorin and company had entered Mirkwood, Gandalf had warned them to stick to the footpath and that if they wandered into the woods, they'd likely never make it out alive.

However, what Gandalf *hadn't* known was that in recent years, heavy rains and floods had turned the eastern end of the forest path into a wide, treacherous swamp many travelers had perished trying to cross. Bilbo and the dwarves *had* needed to stay on the track *most* of the way across Mirkwood—just as they had done—but it had also been vital that they turn north off the path when they did. Only the river that ran under the elves' cavern offered a way out of Mirkwood.

Their failure (wandering off the path) and misfortune (being imprisoned by the elves) were, in the end, a stroke of good fortune.

Tolkien invented a new word—*eucatastrophe*—to describe such unexpected, propitious turns of events. A *catastrophe* (literally an "overturning") was a term used in Greek plays to signify the end of the story, the conclusion of the plot. "*Eu*" is the Greek word for *good*, so a *eu*catastrophe, by contrast, was "a sudden and miraculous grace,"[47] or a happy ending that overturned a tragedy. Hobbits delighted in just such stories, and they eagerly listened to Gandalf tell tales about "the unexpected luck of widows' sons."[48]

But are there really such things as *eu*catastrophes, situations where tragedies and catastrophes unexpectedly work out for the best? Yes.

In the Bible, Joseph's ten older brothers hated him so much that one day while they were out in the pastures, they seized him and sold him to a caravan plodding down to Egypt. Once there, Joseph was forced to work as a slave for years, and just when things started to look up, he was accused of a crime he hadn't committed and thrown in prison, where he languished for several more years.

Then one day, Joseph was abruptly summoned from jail to interpret Pharaoh's dreams. Joseph told Pharaoh that his visions were a warning that seven years of good harvests would be followed by seven years of terrible famine. As a result of this warning, Joseph was promoted to governor over the entire land. The day came when the famine hit Egypt and the surrounding countries, but Egypt was prepared, having taken Joseph's advice to store up grain for such an event.

When his brothers arrived from Canaan to buy grain, Joseph eventually revealed himself to them and had his entire family move to Egypt. As he later told them, "You intended to harm me, but God intended it for good to accomplish what is now being done, the saving of many lives" (Genesis 50:20 NIV).

The greatest eucatastrophe of history happened to Jesus Christ. Despite the fact that He went everywhere doing good, His own people rejected Him; He was betrayed by one of His disciples; He was falsely accused and imprisoned; He was crucified; and His dead body was laid in a tomb. Yet this catastrophe was overturned by the greatest happy ending of all time, when Jesus Christ was raised from the dead, proving definitively that He was the Son of God and the long-awaited Messiah. As it turned out, it was necessary for Him to suffer *and* to triumph. Jesus himself asked, "Ought not the Christ to have suffered these things and to enter into His glory?" (Luke 24:26 NKJV).

Down through the ages to the present day, God has continued to bring victories from defeat—and to turn catastrophes into eucatastrophes.

Paul told the early Christians, "And we know that all things work together for good to those who love God, to those who are the called according to His purpose" (Romans 8:28 NKJV). Not everything that happens to us *is* good in and of itself, but God can make even the worst things work together for our good in the end. God knows every detail of our circumstances. He knows it's extremely difficult to be facing what appears to be the end, to be suffering for our mistakes and failures with no apparent way to set things right and reach our intended goal. But it's not the end—even when the drama has reached its apparent conclusion and the credits begin to roll. God can mend our broken dreams. He can bring order and meaning out of our messes and disasters.

God is in control, and, like Bilbo, we may reach our goals by the only road that was any good after all.

39

Pleasant Legends, Potent Prophecies

Some sang too that Thror and Thrain would come back one day and gold would flow in rivers. . . . But this pleasant legend did not much affect their daily business.

THE HOBBIT, CHAPTER 10

E sgaroth (commonly called Laketown) was a large wooden settlement resting atop posts in the waters of Long Lake. The town was still prosperous and handled trade between the wood-elves in the northeast and the great gardens of Dorwinion to the south. But in days of old, when Thror had ruled the fabulously wealthy dwarf kingdom of Erebor, Esgaroth had been *far* richer. Fleets of boats, some filled with gold, had traveled up and down the rivers.

After the dragon had decimated Erebor, Thror and his son Thrain, together with Thorin, had apparently first retreated to Laketown. There, with his beard still singed by dragon fire, Thror had vowed to return to his home and treasure. This was more than a promise; it was a prophecy, and when Bilbo and the dwarves were taken to the great hall where the Master of the town sat feasting, Thorin boldly shouted, "I return!"[49]

Years earlier, the townspeople had composed songs describing this event, so when Thorin proclaimed that he was come to fulfill "the homecoming spoken of old,"[50] people began singing the old songs. They were especially thrilled because, according to the lyrics, the rivers would once again run with gold, bringing prosperity to *them* as well.

The Master didn't believe the songs, and he was preoccupied with trade and collecting tolls on cargoes passing through. Truth be told, most people hadn't really taken the songs seriously but considered them mere pleasant legends with little or no bearing on their lives. Even those who actually believed the dwarf-king would *eventually* return hadn't expected it to happen in *their* days—so they were totally unprepared when Thorin showed up.

Does this sound familiar? We believers say we believe Jesus is coming again, and many of us insist emphatically that we're living in Earth's final hours and that Jesus could come at any instant. We say His kingdom will be set up soon, a kingdom where truth and righteousness are far more important than any material gain we may enjoy in this present life. But do we *live* like this is what we believe? Do our daily choices reflect the priorities we should have? Or do our lifestyles tend to indicate that we believe this world is going to go on, well. . .forever?

Jesus was aware of such all-too-human tendencies, so He advised His disciples: "Be dressed for service and keep your lamps burning, as though you were waiting for your master to return. . . . Then you will be ready to open the door and let him in the moment he arrives and knocks. The servants who are ready and waiting for his return will be rewarded" (Luke 12:35–37 NLT).

Jesus' admonition still applies today. He has promised to return, and He tells us to continue faithfully serving Him while we await His second coming.

Many of us, although we certainly believe in heaven, are so focused on this present world that we lose sight of the fact that heaven is our ultimate home—the place where we'll live with God and our loved ones forever, the place where all of our good deeds will be rewarded and all of our sacrifices and losses for Christ's sake will be reimbursed. Jesus put a great emphasis on this, but unless we truly *grasp* it, it really won't affect the way we go about our daily lives.

And if we don't faithfully live our lives according to Jesus' teachings, we won't receive a full reward when He returns.

Jesus said, "Do not lay up for yourselves treasures on earth, where moth and rust destroy and where thieves break in and steal; but lay up for yourselves treasures in heaven" (Matthew 6:19–20 NKJV). We accumulate treasures in heaven by obeying Jesus' command to love God and to love one another, by living honestly, by giving generously, and by doing good to others whenever we have opportunity.

It's like preparing to move to another state and making the down payment on a home there ahead of time. In anticipation of our move, we send our valuables on ahead, open up a new bank account, and begin transferring our money. Jesus summed up this idea, saying, "For where your treasure is, there your heart will be also" (Matthew 6:21 NKJV).

Instead of living as if heaven were merely some pleasant legend and focusing on our bank account here on earth, we must realize we're only in this life for a short time—and that our *real* home, our eternal home, is God's kingdom. When we have that firmly in mind, we begin living a life that pleases God.

40
Doubting the Dragon

Other folk were far away; and some of the
younger people in the town openly doubted the
existence of any dragon in the mountain.
THE HOBBIT, CHAPTER 10

It had been 171 years since Smaug had attacked the dwarf kingdom of Erebor and set the town of Dale ablaze. The destruction and loss of life had been tremendous and were indelibly burned into the memories of long-lived dwarves like Thorin and Balin, who'd *been* there but who'd escaped the devastation. They *knew* the dragon was real because they'd seen him and personally witnessed his destructive power.

Although the story had been handed down through the generations of men at Laketown, none of those now living had been alive at the time of the attack. Only the very oldest men, in their youth, had even *seen* the dragon flying. Ever since that cataclysmic night, there had been no further dragon attacks. For over a century, there had been no sightings nor, in fact, any sign that a dragon even existed. Therefore, some of the younger people doubted there'd even *been* a dragon but reasoned that the destruction of Erebor and Dale had been the result of some great fire.

Far away to the south, in the Shire, hobbits like Bilbo had heard about dragons, as well, and believed in them. But the more earthly minded hobbits felt that folk were better off focusing on practical matters like cabbages and potatoes—which were better for them anyway. A hobbit named Ted Sandyman summed up this view of dragons when he stated, "I heard tell of them when I was a youngster, but there's no call to believe in them now."[51]

And dragons *don't* actually exist and never have existed, *have* they? No—at least not in the natural realm, in *this* physical reality—although great and terrifying monsters *have* existed in Earth's distant past. (Job chapter 41 describes a creature called "Leviathan," which bears a striking resemblance to a fire-breathing dragon.) However, the Bible tells us that at least one dragon dwells in the spiritual dimension.

When Tolkien described dragons in Middle-earth, he was unambiguous in describing them as evil. He told no tales about "good" dragons. Every dragon that appeared down through the ages—and they were legion, from Glaurung to Smaug—was an arch-villain, a foe of all that was good, a deceiver and a corrupter of the innocent, and a destroyer of home and property. This view was rooted in Tolkien's Christian worldview, in which the devil is described as "an enormous red dragon. . .that ancient serpent called the devil, or Satan, who leads the whole world astray" (Revelation 12:3, 9 NIV).

It's a strange thing, but many people today, while they believe in God, have their doubts about whether the devil— the very personification of evil—actually exists. Many modern people view belief in the devil as childish and primitive. Almost all the world's evil, they reason, can be explained as a result of either the selfish instincts within man's heart or of natural forces. All diseases, they argue, have strictly natural causes, and people are deceived not by cunning, evil spiritual beings, but by their own stupidity. The Bible warns against such potentially fatal skepticism: "Stay alert! Watch out for your great enemy, the devil. He prowls around like a roaring lion, looking for someone to devour" (1 Peter 5:8 NLT).

You can hardly watch out for an enemy you don't believe even exists.

On the other hand, it's not healthy to become too fixated on Satan's power. Some people fear the devil and forget that we have power over him through Jesus' name. The apostle John declares, "For this purpose the Son of God was manifested, that He might destroy the works of the devil" (1 John 3:8 NKJV). We're certainly not greater than the ancient serpent, our archenemy—but Jesus *is*, and through His death on the cross He destroyed him who had the power of death, the devil. Jesus triumphed over all the power of the enemy (Hebrews 2:14; Colossians 2:15), and if we stand strong in the authority of His name, we can, too.

The townspeople of Esgaroth had at first been inspired by the ancient prophecies about Thorin and were delighted that they were about to come true. After all, here was Thorin—come to fulfill them! However, when they escorted the dwarves north into the wilderness to the edge of the Desolation of Smaug, they found that "it was easier to believe in the dragon and less easy to believe in Thorin in these wild parts."[52] Why? Because when they saw a land utterly destroyed and made desolate by the dragon, they feared his power—and forgot the power of the prophecies.

We should never belittle the existence of the devil and his demons. On the other hand, we must remember that Jesus said, "I give unto you power. . .over all the power of the enemy" (Luke 10:19 KJV). As sons and daughters of God, we have authority through Jesus' name over the forces of darkness.

41

When False Hope Dies

*They were alone in the perilous waste without hope
of further help. . . . None of them had much spirit left.*
THE HOBBIT, CHAPTER 11

The dwarves had been greatly encouraged in Lake-town. Brand-new songs had been written foretelling the sudden death of the dragon and the restoration of the King under the Mountain. Everywhere the dwarves went, people had cheered. Thorin had strutted around town as if the kingdom were already his and Smaug were already dead. Now, however, they'd arrived at Lonely Mountain, and evidence of the destructive power of the dragon was everywhere. As the reality of the situation sunk in, their pride failed, the song lyrics fled, and their spirits fell.

They realized how powerless they were against such a foe. Part of this feeling of despair was to be expected. After all, they'd understood from the beginning that there wasn't "any real hope of destroying Smaug. There was no hope."[53] They'd known they were engaged in a desperate venture and that some of them might not survive. Their stay in Laketown had fueled hopes of an easy victory, but now grim reality rushed back into their minds with such force that they were overcome with hopelessness and confusion.

Instead of immediately heading for the western slopes to look for the secret door, Thorin sent scouts to check out the gate at the southern slope. He apparently wanted to see if the situation was as grim as it seemed. Seeing the ruins of the once-proud town of Dale, however, confirmed to the dwarves that, yes, the situation *was* grim. It also reminded them that there were no armies to help them now. They were utterly on their own.

This discouraged them so much that when they returned to camp, they didn't feel like doing *anything*. It took Bilbo to urge them to look for the secret door.

Sometimes, like Thorin, we're fully aware we're up against a truly monstrous obstacle, a seemingly unsolvable problem. We've spent more than enough time analyzing the situation from every possible angle, seeking a solution;

and the reality of how desperate our situation is isn't lost on us. We know that no efforts we muster can resolve the situation.

When a situation is impossible, it's good to understand that fact clearly. Doing so makes us realize that we can't hope to succeed on our own, that it's *beyond* any solutions we can come up with. This realization will drive us to God, and we will look to Him to help us because we know we truly *need* His help.

In King Jehoshaphat's days, messengers brought the alarming news that three enemy nations (Edom, Ammon, and Moab) had joined forces and invaded Judah. The invaders had swept over the southern defenses of the kingdom, and Judah was about to be overrun and annihilated. Jehoshaphat was afraid—and rightfully so. He prayed, "O LORD God. . .in Your hand is there not power and might, so that no one is able to withstand You?" Jehoshaphat then admitted how powerless he was, saying, "O our God, will You not judge them? For we have no power against this great multitude that is coming against us; nor do we know what to do, but our eyes are upon You" (2 Chronicles 20:6, 12 NKJV).

As a result of Jehoshaphat's sincere prayer, God did a miracle and delivered Judah. (You can read the full, amazing story in 2 Chronicles 20.)

How different was Judah's "solution" in Isaiah's day! When Assyria was about to invade their land, they *also* realized how the crisis was beyond their power to deal with. But instead of looking to God, they came up with a happy solution. Need protection? Easy! Ask Big Daddy Egypt! They made a military alliance with Pharaoh, for which God rebuked them, saying, "For without consulting me, you have gone down to Egypt for help. You have put your trust in Pharaoh's protection. You have tried to hide in his shade. But by trusting Pharaoh, you will be humiliated. . . . He will not help you" (Isaiah 30:2–3, 5 NLT).

Sure enough, Egypt couldn't help Judah but was *itself* soon overrun by Assyria.

When we face a desperate situation, it's not good to allow overly optimistic friends to convince us that "everything will work out somehow" or that we'll surely be able to figure out some solution. When we do that, we set ourselves up for disappointment, because the bottom will eventually fall out of our unrealistic optimism, and we'll slam back into reality with even greater impact.

It's always best to honestly face the facts. The sooner we do that, the sooner we'll turn to God and pray, "We don't know what to do, but our eyes are upon You."

When we admit to ourselves that we simply don't know what to do, it may almost seem like we're giving up—and, in a sense, we are. . .at least on our own ability. But when we look to God, we acknowledge His power and trust Him to come up with a solution we could never even have imagined.

42

Waiting for an Open Door

A door five feet high and three broad was outlined,
and slowly without a sound swung inwards.
THE HOBBIT, CHAPTER 11

According to Thror's map, the secret door was located in the upper end of a long, narrow valley—but it took Bilbo and the dwarves many days of searching to find it. There, above a cliff, set in the western side of the mountain, was a flat wall of stone. They had found the secret door. . . but still couldn't see it. Thorin had the *key*, but no keyhole was visible. They eagerly pushed against the stone, but it wouldn't budge. They tried to chip away an opening but couldn't make a dent. The dwarves recited every password they could remember, but nothing would open it.

How had they forgotten Thror's clearly written instructions?

The door would only open under certain specific circumstances. It had to be Durin's Day—the last New Moon before winter. Furthermore, they had to hear a thrush "knocking." Only then would the last glint of daylight reveal the keyhole. But all of this had slipped the dwarves' minds. They'd been so eager to open the door that they couldn't be bothered with the instructions. Instead, they sat for days, trying to think of what to do. Read the instructions? How could they? The moon-runes were now invisible. And *what* had they said anyway?

Bilbo was staring toward the setting sun one day when he noticed the slender crescent of a New Moon. Just then he heard a knocking sound; behind him was a large thrush with a snail in its mouth, cracking its shell against a stone. Bilbo excitedly called the dwarves together, and they waited. Sure enough, the last shaft of sunlight struck the wall; the thrush gave a loud trill; and a stone chip fell away, revealing the keyhole. Thorin thrust in the key and. . .the door opened!

You not only have to be in the right *place* but you also have to be there at the right *time*.

The Bible often speaks of people encountering *closed* or *open* doors. An "open door" is a unique opportunity God gives His people—a way into or out of a certain situation at a certain, precise time. For example, Jesus said to the Christians of Philadelphia, "I have set before you an open door, and no one can shut it" (Revelation 3:8 NKJV), and Paul said that "when I came to Troas to preach Christ's gospel. . .a door was opened to me by the Lord" (2 Corinthians 2:12 NKJV).

However, the Bible warns that we will also come up against *closed* doors, where situations seem impossible and there appears to be no way through them. So what can we do? At times like this, Paul asked other Christians to pray that God would open a door (Colossians 4:2–3) because he knew there was no way he could open the door by his own efforts. For example, when he set out to preach the gospel in the Roman province of Asia, the Holy Spirit didn't permit him to go there because it wasn't yet time (Acts 16:6). When it *was* time, however, God opened a "great door" in Ephesus, the most important city in the region (1 Corinthians 16:8–9).

Sometimes we, like the dwarves, want doors to open at our command—exactly when we want them opened. After all, we have the key to the situation, so shouldn't the keyhole be waiting in plain sight? Shouldn't we be able to open the door at the time of our choosing? We're there, on location, ready to do the job. We're primed and ready to go. Why wait any longer? Such zeal, however, is often little more than haughty impatience.

To be fair, we're often driven by genuine needs. You're moving and need a good home to become available—and *soon*. You've graduated from university with a degree, and now need a job in that field to open up. You desperately need a breakthrough in business.

Whatever your situation, you're ready and waiting for a door to be opened. Instead, like the dwarves, you find yourself up against a blank wall. At times like these, the solution sometimes comes by a chance meeting with a key person or a random phone call from a friend who just happens to have heard that so-and-so's brother-in-law has exactly what you need. When that happens, you've just had a divine appointment, and the beauty is often that it came so unexpectedly, so effortlessly.

When you come up against a closed door, however, and it *doesn't* automatically open, and none of your efforts can give you a way through it, then you do well to pray and trust that God will open it. . .in His time. If you're at the right place at the right time, God can make things turn out far better than you could possibly have managed on your own. If you have a little patience, you'll save yourself a lot of time and frustration in the long run.

Are you waiting for a miracle? Pray for God to open a way.

43

Called Upon Yet Again

"Now who is coming with me?" He did not expect
a chorus of volunteers, so he was not disappointed.
THE HOBBIT, CHAPTER 12

How smugly self-confident the dwarves had been only a few months earlier. When Gandalf cautioned them on the dangers of confronting Smaug directly, Thorin informed him that he was not instructing novices. He boasted, "Dwarves have had more dealings with dragons than most."[54] And when Gandalf had tried to talk them into bringing a hobbit along on their quest, Gloin had openly mocked the Shire-folk, saying they'd be afraid of even a newly hatched baby dragon.[55]

Now, however, as Bilbo prepared to go down the passage to encounter the monster and asked who was coming with him, only Fili and Kili shuffled awkwardly. The others didn't even bother being embarrassed. Only the elderly Balin agreed to go *part*way down the passage with the hobbit. So much for their vast experience with dragons!

Were Bilbo to recover their plunder, the dwarves, of course, intended to reward him beyond his wildest dreams. And if he died trying, they had solemnly pledged to cover his funeral costs. You have to give them that much.

And, frankly, Bilbo should have known better than to ask. No dwarf *could* come with him. He was the soft-footed burglar, the only one who could slip in and out of the dragon's chamber—and he was the one with an invisible ring. So why *did* he ask? Because he was tired of constantly being called upon. He'd repeatedly had to rescue them, lead the way, and make decisions. He wanted one of *them* to step up to the plate for a change. Where was Thorin's leadership?

Nevertheless, the hobbit realized that he was the burglar, and—come to think of it—he *didn't* want any of them coming along and making a lot of dwarvish racket. Thus it was that Bilbo headed down the passage alone.

Being constantly called upon to help someone can get a little tiring after a while. You feel like you're being taken for granted, and, like Bilbo, you begin to wonder, *Why don't they help themselves? Why don't they ask someone else to help them for a change? Why does it always have to be me to get them out of their jams?*

This is particularly true when you have specialized skills—like if you're a mechanic in a family where everyone's cars constantly break down, or if you're a handyman whose friends are non-handymen with leaky toilets. Or you have a stable job, and the same person keeps borrowing money from you again and again. At first, you don't mind helping. After all, you know that you're helping people do something that they can't do themselves; they're effusive in their thanks; and it's nice that your talents and generosity are recognized. You do your good deed for the day, and you feel good about it.

But when it goes on and on, when you *keep* being called upon to do good deeds for the same people, month after month, their gratitude can begin to wear thin. They can, like the dwarves, take off their hoods and sincerely pledge themselves "in your debt" all they want, but you can become a little peeved that they always depend on you to do things that, really, they *could* (theoretically) learn to do themselves. Or if they searched a little—say, in the Yellow Pages—they could find someone *else* to ask.

Nevertheless, Jesus advised that "whoever compels you

to go one mile, go with him two. Give to him who asks you, and from him who wants to borrow from you do not turn away" (Matthew 5:41–42 NKJV). Certainly Jesus intended that you should cheerfully go out of your way to help others—even when it's inconvenient. But notice He *didn't* say that if someone asks you to go one mile with him, that you should volunteer to go twenty. It's good to be generous, with your time and your money, but you need to know your limits. If you don't, you'll suffer burnout and won't be around to help anyone else who desperately needs your assistance.

Those who *really* need your help—the kind of people you're *not* supposed to turn a blind eye to—are those in hopeless situations without the means to help themselves: "Pure and genuine religion in the sight of God the Father means caring for orphans and widows in their distress" (James 1:27 NLT). However, it's a different story with able-bodied people who *can* help themselves.

And sometimes, even when you're perfectly willing to help, it's not simply inconvenient but actually impossible. There's an important distinction, however, between being *unable* to help and being *unwilling*.

Be willing to help those who really need it. After all, there may come a time when you need someone's help, and it may not be convenient for *them*.

44

Facing the Dragon

Going on from there was the bravest thing he ever did. . . .
He fought the real battle in that tunnel alone,
before he ever saw the vast danger that lay in wait.
THE HOBBIT, CHAPTER 12

Balin accompanied Bilbo down the first part of the passage, but Bilbo was on his own after that. At this point, Mr. Baggins slipped on his invisible ring. He was a much bolder hobbit by this time. . . . Nevertheless, it was with *huge* misgivings that he continued down deep into the bowels of the mountain. He called himself a total fool for ever having volunteered for this quest. He wished he could turn back and just leave the dragon with all his ill-gotten gold. But he'd committed himself. He *had* to go on. . .so he did.

It was a long, long, *long* passage. Bilbo entered it shortly after sundown and didn't return until midnight. He was creeping as quietly (and therefore as slowly) as he could, so he had more than enough time during his dismal descent to think about the immense danger he was heading into. As he approached the end of the passage, he began to feel very warm. Then he saw a red glow ahead. Next, he smelled sulfuric vapors. Finally, he began to hear the ominous gurgling rumble of the monster snoring. He hadn't yet seen Smaug, but all his other senses were kicking in with the same message: *The dragon is home!*

Bilbo froze in his tracks.

Any hope he'd had that Smaug might not be there vanished—replaced by a certainty that the dragon was not only present and accounted for but also every bit as powerful and vicious as the tales made him out to be. Mr. Baggins stood unmoving for only a short time before continuing, but during those moments he fought the biggest mental battle of his life. Then, his mind made up, he continued.

Sometimes we talk ourselves into doing something extraordinarily out of character—such as bungee-jumping off a bridge when we're afraid of heights or giving a speech when we're deathly afraid of public speaking. Later, we find ourselves poised behind the railing or standing at the edge of the curtain as they call our name. . .for the second time. But in such cases, although we fear those things, we're also aware that they *won't* actually kill us. For example, we know that—statistically speaking—even flying is not that dangerous—and we're *not* actually likely to die in the dentist's chair.

There's a difference between being afraid of something when we know the odds of it killing us are actually negligible and being afraid of something we know could actually harm us.

In the days of the Persian Empire, a draconian law stated that anyone who entered the king's inner court uninvited was to be executed. It didn't help that a plot had recently been uncovered in which palace guards had conspired to assassinate the king. Yet Queen Esther *had* to get in to see him. Time was of the essence, so she couldn't wait for an invitation. A powerful enemy, Haman, was planning to kill all the Jews from one end of the Persian Empire to the other, and the king was the only one who could thwart him. Esther was the queen, but she had apparently fallen badly out of favor with his highness her husband, because he hadn't called her in to see him for (would you believe?) *one full month*.

What was Esther to do? Did she simply let her

people die? No. . .she couldn't do *that*. But she also knew that unless the king made an exception to his rule and held out his royal scepter—indicating that her life was to be spared—she was walking to her death. (They must've been going through a *major* relationship crisis if she had serious doubts he'd even do *that*!) Finally, she made up her mind and said, "Though it is against the law, I will go in to see the king. If I must die, I must die" (Esther 4:16 NLT).

Did Esther pause a moment before opening the door to the king's court? Probably so. But she'd just finished praying for three days and working through her fears, so she took the plunge. (And she *lived*, by the way, which shows there's hope for even the rockiest relationships.)

Bilbo had apparently reached the same conclusion: "If I die, I die." Apparently, during his long, long, long walk down the passage, he thought the matter through and realized this was something he simply *had* to do. So in the end, he paused only briefly before continuing.

There may be times when we're called upon to make such life-threatening stands as well—or at least stands with potentially serious consequences. If we've thought the matter through ahead of time and know what our convictions are, we won't hesitate. . .at least not for more than a moment.

45

It Comes with the Territory

*They realized that dangers of this kind were inevitable
in dealing with such a guardian, and that it
was no good giving up their quest yet.*
THE HOBBIT, CHAPTER 12

As he entered the subterranean chamber, Bilbo saw the dragon sprawled atop a great heap of treasure, sleeping. He was at first overawed by the sight of the beast, but then, snapping to his senses, he seized a heavy golden cup and lugged it back up the tunnel. When he arrived at the doorway, the dwarves praised him repeatedly and began to talk about how soon *all* the treasure would be theirs.

Then Smaug awoke and noticed that the cup was

missing. (Talk about an eye for detail!) Bellowing with rage, he issued from the front gate. Bilbo and the dwarves had barely scrambled inside the passage when Smaug swooped down, blistering the slopes with his burning breath. The dragon circled the mountain all night searching for them, but he never saw them.

At sunrise, Smaug returned to his lair, and the dwarves' fears subsided. They had a long discussion on the best way to get rid of Smaug but, of course, couldn't think of anything that would actually *work*. But, despite their desperate situation—trapped inside the tunnel, most of their supplies gone—they refused to give up. They'd known from the beginning that reclaiming treasure from a dragon had its risks.

The dwarves had become deeply discouraged before, "yet they would not give up and go away."[56] Despite becoming dispirited again and again, they had persevered. Part of it was the fact that the dragon had their gold and they wanted it back. It was partly because the dragon had slain their families and friends, and they wanted justice. It was also partly because hope dies hard in dwarvish hearts, and though they didn't have the *slightest* clue how they'd get rid of Smaug, they still hoped it'd happen. Another thing: they'd already suffered so many hardships in their quest, and if they had given up then, all their privations and pain would've been for nothing.

In the New Testament, when the Christians of Galatia were beginning to get off track and give up, Paul asked, "Have you suffered so many things in vain—if indeed it was in vain?" (Galatians 3:4 NKJV).

Many Christians in Rome ended up at the same crossroads. They'd previously stood strong despite suffering and persecution, yet now they were facing a *new* test and wavered in their faith. So God urged them, "Remember those earlier days after you had received the light, when you endured in a great conflict full of suffering." He reminded them how they'd been slandered, persecuted, even imprisoned for what they believed—but they hadn't given up. So He encouraged them to hang on a little longer, saying, "So do not throw away your confidence; it will be richly rewarded. You need to persevere so that when you have done the will of God, you will receive what he has promised" (Hebrews 10:32, 35–36 NIV).

At times we, too, feel we can't go on much longer. We've been through a lot, we've stood strong through the years, and we've come a long way. We *were* making it, but frankly we were feeling a little worn out. Then, suddenly, we're blindsided by an accident, the loss of a major client, a relationship mess, or something else we have no idea how to deal with. We sit with our head in our hands, barely able to pray. *Wasn't God supposed to be with us to protect us?* we think. *Why did He allow this to happen? Is this some test? If it is, we surely didn't need this!*

We know we're near the end of our quest, almost in sight of our goal, but it all seems so hard at this point. Our hope of heaven is so distant and so overshadowed by our present trials and temptations that it barely seems worth focusing on. We feel like dropping our faith by the wayside.

This is when we need the tenacity of the dwarves. Like them, we simply must refuse to give up and go away.

Fortunately, as discouraged as we feel, we usually *don't* give up completely. Even when we're angry at God for allowing us some misfortune, we usually don't abandon our faith. But oftentimes, like the dwarves, we sullenly hunker down inside a mountain and do nothing. We stop going to church, we lose our desire to pray, and we don't read our Bible. In short, we take a "time-out" from God. Yet the issue all along isn't God. It's the devil who's fighting us. So we must fight back—against Satan and against despair.

Yes, it's one honkin' huge dragon we're up against. But we *knew* that when we started out.

When we feel discouraged or defeated, we need to remind ourselves of our earlier days, when we endured great suffering because we believed it would be worth it all in the end. And it was! And it *still* is worth fighting for. God will see to it that all our suffering is rewarded. . .if only we hang on.

46

Reaching Your Potential

Already they had come to respect little Bilbo.
Now he had become the real leader in their adventure.
THE HOBBIT, CHAPTER 12

The dwarves became so upset with their predicament that they began to blame Smaug's fiery attack on the hobbit. After all, they grumbled, if Bilbo hadn't removed the golden cup, the dragon wouldn't now be out to kill them. Bilbo retorted that he was the burglar and had simply done his job. His job description did *not* include killing the dragon.

Bilbo was right, of course. So when Thorin apologized and asked him what they should do, Bilbo made a daring suggestion: he would sneak back down the passage to see what Smaug was up to and to find out if the dragon had a weak spot. It was a widely known bit of dragon lore that although the great reptiles were covered head to tail with impenetrable scales, they had a soft spot. (Bilbo did indeed discover that Smaug had a large soft patch at his left breast, over his heart—and this knowledge eventually led directly to the dragon's death.)

It was a dangerous, desperate gamble, but what else could they do?

Even though Thorin was king, Bilbo had now emerged as *de facto* leader. He hadn't seemed like much of a leader while he was quivering in fear back in the Shire, but he'd proved since then that he had the right stuff, and the dwarves now looked up to him. Very importantly, Bilbo himself had accepted his role. He realized that *his* analysis of situations had repeatedly provided solutions and that *his* leadership had saved their lives time and again. If it'd been up to Thorin, they'd all be dead. . .or still in prison.

In fact, Thorin had all but abdicated his role. Of *course* Bilbo had to lead.

The Bible recounts a scenario very much like this one. One day, a monster of a man named Goliath began to defy the armies of Israel. He was over nine feet tall, and, like Smaug, he was plastered with armor: "He wore a bronze helmet, and his bronze coat of mail weighed 125 pounds. He also wore bronze leg armor, and. . .his armor bearer walked ahead of him carrying a shield" (1 Samuel 17:5–7 NLT). In addition, Goliath was armed with a bronze javelin, a massive spear, and a great iron sword.

Goliath challenged the Israelites to pick their best, strongest warrior to come out and fight him. Here is what was at stake: if Goliath lost, the Philistines would become the Israelites' slaves, but if he won, the Israelites would become slaves to the Philistines.

Not a man in the Israelite army dared challenge Goliath—not even King Saul, who was a veteran warrior and "taller than any of the people from his shoulders upward" (1 Samuel 10:23 NKJV). That's when David, armed with only a shepherd's staff and a sling, stepped forward.

David rejected traditional battle weapons and refused to wear body armor. He knew that he didn't stand a chance against the giant using conventional weapons, so he ran toward Goliath, swung his sling furiously, and hurled a stone at a "soft spot" in the giant's armor—his forehead. And down the giant went. David not only led his people to victory that day, but later went on to become king of Israel.

You're probably not destined to become the leader of a dwarf expedition *or* the ruler of Israel. You may not end up as leader of *any* group, in fact. But you have the potential to rise up in time of need. You have your particular abilities and areas of expertise that help you advise on the wisest course of action. Or you may offer an innovative plan that solves a baffling problem. This holds true whether you're a student, an accountant, a computer technician, or a construction worker. . .or a school teacher, a fireman, or a secretary.

You may not even bear the title of "leader," but everyone will know that in an hour of need, you were the *real* leader. You may not be called upon to lead for long, but when your moment comes, you must be willing to accept that role—especially if those in charge are unwilling or unable to do the job.

You may not feel like much of a leader. . .but how is a leader *supposed* to feel anyway? Hey, even Moses, as great a leader as he turned out to be, at first didn't think he had it in him (Exodus 3:7–12; 4:10–15). Many great men and women have felt utterly incapable of leading, but they rose to the occasion and simply did what they were supposed to do.

Perhaps you can identify with mild-mannered Mr. Baggins. Apart from his battle with the spiders, he was not a leader in any military sense. Most of his leadership abilities resided in the fact that he gave wise advice—and we can *all* do that. . .at least when the conversation rolls around to an area in which we have some knowledge.

Add a bit of courage and initiative to your good advice, and you can lead.

47

The Effect of Dragon-Talk

Now a nasty suspicion began to grow in his mind. . . .
That is the effect that dragon-talk has on the inexperienced.
THE HOBBIT, CHAPTER 12

Dragons are a fascinating topic today, even though we know they're mythological. But can you imagine how much they'd be discussed and studied in a world where they really existed? As Tolkien observed, "It does not do to leave a live dragon out of your calculations, if you live near him."[57] Of course, there's no record of a dragon marauding in the Shire, so any knowledge hobbits had of such creatures was secondhand.

Unlike most hobbits, who usually busied themselves

with practical matters, Bilbo was an avid reader and had gone out of his way to talk with strangers. So he had above-average knowledge of dragon-lore. This now served him well, for as soon as he entered Smaug's chamber, the dragon detected his presence and addressed him. Fortunately, Bilbo knew it was important to be polite to a dragon and to flatter it. It was also very important—if you wanted to avoid giving direct answers—to speak to a dragon in riddles, so he did precisely that.

Just the same, Smaug was incredibly cunning and, putting the clues together, figured out that Bilbo had traveled there with thirteen dwarves, that he was their professional burglar, and that he had been promised a one-fourteenth share. Smaug then set to work to create suspicion in Bilbo's mind, and it worked. Bilbo began to seriously wonder whether Thorin was planning to cheat him in the end.

Smaug's talk had another effect: Bilbo had come to the dragon as the selfless, courageous leader of the expedition. The dwarves hadn't compelled him; he had voluntarily risked his life. Smaug's accusations, however, took Bilbo's eyes off helping the dwarves survive and focused them on his own supposed grievance. He went from being a hero to a mercenary. Fortunately, Bilbo pushed his doubts out of his mind for the time being, finished his mission, and escaped back up the passage. . .*barely*.

There is a great deal of dragon-talk in the real world as well. Solomon observed, "A perverse person stirs up conflict, and a gossip separates close friends" (Proverbs 16:28 NIV). Many of us know this from personal experience; we've seen busybodies with busy tongues destroy close friendships. That's why the Law of Moses commands: "Do not spread slanderous gossip among your people" (Leviticus 19:16 NLT). Or as another translation (the New King James Version) says: "You shall not go about as a talebearer among your people." The image in this verse is of a person walking about an entire neighborhood, spreading tales— blabbing about someone's personal matters simply because it's such a juicy conversation piece.

That's malicious, *idle* gossip, and it's bad enough. But malicious, *intentional* slander is quite something else. That's genuine dragon-talk, and its purpose is to destroy its target. The apostle John had a vision of a great red dragon pursuing a woman (symbolic of God's people) in the wilderness, and the dragon spewed a great torrent of water out of his mouth with the intent of sweeping her away (Revelation 12:13–15). Many Bible commentators believe that the flood pouring out of the dragon's mouth symbolizes a flood of vicious words.

For people engaging in character assassination, the truth itself is irrelevant. If a bit of truth mixed in makes the story more believable, all the better. But if not, a bold lie will do. The Bible says of people who do such things that their "tongue devises destruction, like a sharp razor, working deceitfully" (Psalm 52:2 NKJV).

We know not to gossip, and we certainly know better than to spread slander. But how do we respond when we hear slanderous gossip about family or friends? Like Bilbo, we may not initially be able to prevent a "nasty suspicion" from forming in our minds—but do we strive to remain loyal to those we care about? Do we give them the benefit of the doubt until we're able to directly ask them about the matter? Or do we burn with indignation at the supposed injustice and confront them angrily?

When Bilbo later asked Thorin about what he had been told, the dwarf-king answered the hobbit straightforwardly and assured him that he intended to keep his word. And Bilbo (mostly) believed him. Friendships meant a great deal to him, and he was inclined to trust.

Some of us are by nature more suspicious than Bilbo, however. We don't even need to *hear* gossip about someone. We're quite capable—all on our own, or with a little "help" from the devil—of suspecting the worst motives in someone. But unwarranted suspicions cause discord and divisions, and they are more often wrong than right.

Once we allow words of suspicion and doubt to be

sown in our minds, they grow into life-sucking weeds. That's why it's important not only to make an effort to disbelieve them but also to bring them to light, resolve them, and then ruthlessly pluck them out of our minds. Otherwise they'll continue to erode our trust and influence our actions.

Beware of dragon-talk, whether it's whispered in your ear or whispered in your mind.

48

A Noble Friend

"It is about our turn to help," said Balin,
"and I am quite willing to go."
THE HOBBIT, CHAPTER 13

The night following his chat with Bilbo, Smaug attacked the secret door, lashing the rock face with his tail. The roof of the upper passage collapsed, burying the door, and the dwarves were trapped. They waited until they couldn't bear it any longer. Since their way out was barred, they crept down the passage to the chamber below. To their surprise, the dragon wasn't there.

They were wary, however, so they sent Bilbo ahead to check things out. The hobbit was all the way across the great hall when his torch went out, and he shouted for the dwarves to help him and bring a light. All they could hear, however, was, "Help!" Thorin grumbled at the request. Though the dwarves were glad Bilbo had rescued *them* time and again, he was, after all, simply contracted to do a job.

Only Balin was actually fond of Bilbo, so when the hobbit called out, he willingly set out to help.

Balin was a fascinating character. Thorin Oakenshield was not the only dwarf of royal blood; Balin was, too, and, as it turned out, he was the noblest dwarf of all. Despite his great age, Balin had very keen eyes and was constantly on lookout duty. Despite his regal heritage and seniority, he didn't deem this beneath his dignity. He was also the most kind-hearted dwarf of them all; after Bilbo's last disastrous encounter with the dragon, Balin had gone out of his way to comfort him.

Balin was a true friend.

Gandalf tells us, "Dwarves understand and approve devotion to friends."[58] Loyalty to friends fits well with the dwarves' clannish worldview. Nevertheless, when most dwarves thought of their friends, they usually thought of other dwarves. They were a closely knit, closed society and rarely had deep friendships outside their kind. Hence, when they bowed and took off their hoods to strangers and pledged, "At your service," it was usually only a polite greeting.

The Bible actually urges us to especially show love to other Christians and to do deeds of kindness for fellow believers. Jesus said, "By this all will know that you are My disciples, if you have love for one another" (John 13:35 NKJV). Paul then added, "Whenever we have the opportunity, we should do good to everyone—especially to those in the family of faith" (Galatians 6:10 NLT). So a special bond of love between Christians is described in the Bible as good and right.

Like the dwarves, however, some Christians tend to form themselves into closely knit, closed societies. They focus on the biblical command to do good to fellow Christians to such an extent that they associate and do business almost solely with other believers. Some have as few non-Christian friends as possible—indeed, some rarely move outside their own church circle.

Loving and spending time with fellow Christians are *good* things—so long as we don't do them to the point where we exclude nonbelievers entirely. When we do that, we isolate ourselves from the world around us.

And that's really no credit to us at all.

Jesus said, "If you love those who love you, what credit is that to you? Even sinners love those who love them. And if you do good to those who are good to you, what credit is that to you? Even sinners do that" (Luke 6:32–33 NIV). Jesus treated people with warmth and kindness, and

He wants us to do the same, even when they're ungrateful and don't respond by doing good back to us. When we do that, it proves that we're "children of the Most High, because he is kind to the ungrateful and wicked" (Luke 6:35 NIV).

Of course, we'll always seek to spend more time with those with whom we're *most* compatible—who share our interests, our life passions, our worldview and values, and our faith. These will be our closest, dearest friends.

Being friendly to all people doesn't mean you'll suddenly become a jolly extrovert when you're an introvert by nature. You don't have to shower greetings on everyone you pass and engage in conversation with total strangers to be friendly. That's *some* people's style, but it may not be yours. God knows that, but He also knows that everyone—even a naturally shy person—has his or her own unique way of reaching out to others and being friendly.

We *start* to prove we're Jesus' followers when we love fellow Christians. But having done that, our next step in proving we belong to God is to love even ungrateful and wicked people—just like God does. If we are friendly toward even the most unlovely, we won't have difficulty moving outside the confines of our social circle and being friendly toward *anybody*.

And that, of course, is the whole idea.

49

A Kingly Gift

"Mr. Baggins!" he cried. "Here is the first payment of your reward! Cast off your old coat and put on this!"
THE HOBBIT, CHAPTER 13

When Bilbo first set out exploring the hall, he was drawn to a spectacular jewel that glowed with inner luminescence and radiantly refracted the light of his torch. It was the Arkenstone of Thrain, the greatest treasure of the House of Durin. Overcome by its enchantment, Bilbo grabbed it and hid it in his pocket. Thorin had, after all, promised Bilbo that he could choose his share of the treasure. Nevertheless, Bilbo's conscience bothered him. Thorin had expressed *his* desire for the Arkenstone, and the hobbit knew Thorin's generous offer had not included this gem.

Despite his glaring faults, Thorin was very generous. As the dwarves began going through the treasure, Thorin spied a coat of chainmail and immediately offered it to the hobbit. If Bilbo had known its worth, he'd have considered himself already paid in full. The corselet was made from an extremely rare metal called *mithril*. In those days, it was worth ten times as much as gold, and later, when there was no more to be found, it became priceless. As Gandalf said, "Its worth was greater than the value of the whole Shire and everything in it."[59] When Gimli heard what Thorin had given Bilbo, he exclaimed, "That was a kingly gift!"[60]

The mithril coat was far more than that. It was vital to the saving of all Middle-earth. Bilbo later lent it to Frodo when he went on his quest to destroy the One Ring, and wearing it saved Frodo's life when he was speared in Moria.[61]

What problems Bilbo caused by taking the Arken-stone! Why did he do it? Possibly he still harbored the suspicion (planted by Smaug) that Thorin was scheming to defraud him of his fair share.

Have you ever been in a situation like that? Convinced that someone was trying to cheat you, have you ever been tempted to take something that didn't belong to you, only to find out later that you'd misjudged that person and that they *had* been fair? (Think of the suspicion and indignation you could have saved yourself if only you'd openly discussed the issue.) Even if you *have* actually been defrauded or underpaid, and the guilty party has no intention of making matters right, you still would not be justified in taking matters into your own hands and "paying yourself." There are mediation and legal recourses for such things, or you can simply let the matter go (1 Corinthians 6:1–7).

Sometimes we make that mistake with *God*. We think He is wrong in withholding good things from us—so we simply *take* what we want.

King David did that, and the results were disastrous.

One day, while David walked on the flat roof of his palace, he saw a gorgeous woman, Bathsheba, bathing in the courtyard below. David was overcome with desire. The fact that Bathsheba belonged to another man didn't stop him, and he sent for her. That one wicked decision led to a series of others, including David's scheme to have Bathsheba's husband killed in battle.

Speaking through the prophet Nathan, God rebuked David for his sin, saying, "I gave you your master's house and your master's wives into your keeping, and gave you the house of Israel and Judah. And if that had been too little, I also would have given you much more!" (2 Samuel 12:8 NKJV).

God had given David the entire kingdom of Israel, and he could have chosen *any* beautiful, unmarried woman for a wife. That was surely *not* too little. But even if it *had* been insufficient, God declared that he would have given David more—much more.

God is *also* willing to "freely give us all things" (Romans 8:32 KJV)—not every Arkenstone or Bathsheba we desire but certainly everything we need. As Jesus said, "If you sinful people know how to give good gifts to your children, how much more will your heavenly Father give good gifts to those who ask him" (Matthew 7:11 NLT). There's no need for us to take what belongs to somebody else. We just need to trust that God will give us what we need.

Yet we often short-circuit God's promised solution by coveting what someone else has and getting frustrated that God hasn't given it to *us*. The apostle James recognized this problem and offered a solution: "You covet but you cannot get what you want, so you quarrel and fight. You do not have because you do not ask God" (James 4:2 NIV).

One reason we neglect to "ask God" is that we're *afraid* of what He'll give us. Some of us think God either has skimped on blessing us in the past or has outright short-changed us. We asked Him for a desirable Arkenstone, but instead He gave us second best—the mithril coat.

The truth is, if we pray sincerely, ask with the right motives, and make our requests in faith, God will give us exactly what we need. Just think of all the good, kingly gifts He's *already* given us!

50

Bard the Grim Bowman

Their captain was Bard, grim-voiced and grim-faced,
whose friends had accused him of prophesying
floods and poisoned fish.
THE HOBBIT, CHAPTER 14

You have to wonder how someone as grim as Bard was descended from Girion, king of Dale, the most fabulous Toy Town of Middle-earth. You see, when Thrain was King of Erebor, "the merry town of Dale"[62] was nestled just south of Lonely Mountain. The dwarves had branched off from metalworking to creating magical toys, which were sold in the toy market of Dale.

So why was Bard so grim? Well, part of it was that he

was born with grim genes. Another reason was that when Smaug attacked Erebor, he also burned down Dale, killed its warriors, and devoured its citizens. Only Girion's wife and son and a few others escaped. Dale was now charred ruins, its memory a source of pain, and Bard was a king in exile.

Bard, however, had risen in the ranks to become captain of the archers of Laketown. The people there admired his courage, but they wished he'd lighten up. He was constantly prophesying about floods, poisoned fish, and other disasters.

Well, what could he *do*?

The ancient biblical prophets were "always warning of war, disaster, and disease" (Jeremiah 28:8 NLT). In those days, warning about coming dangers was simply something men with their eyes open did, though most people didn't appreciate it. "They tell the seers, 'Stop seeing visions!' They tell the prophets, 'Don't tell us what is right. Tell us nice things. Tell us lies'" (Isaiah 30:10 NLT).

This night, when the people saw a burning light rushing their way, Bard instantly knew it was the dragon and urged a call to arms. Immediately the town mobilized. Some men destroyed the bridge that joined Laketown to the shore so the dragon couldn't simply walk into town, spewing out flame. Others soaked the wooden buildings.

Every container was filled with water. The archers gathered under Bard's command.

Then Smaug came in fury, breathing out fire!

When we were kids, it was funny watching the gloomy, pessimistic donkey Eeyore from *Winnie the Pooh*. As adults, however, it's not quite as much fun being around someone who has an Eeyore complex. You know the type: constantly predicting a new economic downturn and mulling over contingency plans; focusing more on the failures of our education system than on its successes; always warning about the deficit, ozone depletion, the next pandemic or superbug, rising food prices, and the looming world water crisis.

But what makes being around people like this so grating is that *much* of the time they're right.

We'll admit that the things they warn us about *are* problems, perhaps *big* ones—but they're not critical yet (at least not that we're aware of), and frankly, it's just depressing to think about them so much.

And yet these new wannabe Jeremiahs just won't stop talking. We want them to lighten up, but they won't. After all, practically speaking, what can we do to fix everything that's broken? If we can't even set aside enough savings to fix our car when it breaks down, how can we fix national or global problems? Besides, if we think too much about these huge problems, we'll only start to despair.

Now, we may not be able to deal with the *whole* world's problems, but we *can* deal with the issues in our local part of it. And we must. "A prudent person foresees danger and takes precautions. The simpleton goes blindly on and suffers the consequences" (Proverbs 22:3 NLT).

We're not going to be held personally responsible for fixing the hole in the ozone layer, but we *can* start with our own lives. After all, we know we need to buy car insurance, homeowner's insurance, and life insurance as a hedge against different kinds of disasters. And we also know we should set aside some savings to tide us over during difficult times. If we just *can't* set aside a significant chunk, well, we can't. . .but we should save what we *can*.

The people of Laketown had enough prudence and foresight—largely due to Bard's influence—to realize that they needed contingency plans. Thus they were able to put them into effect on short notice. Perhaps after the dragon was dead, the land around Dale green and growing and filled with people, and Bard was king, he actually *did* learn to lighten up.

But until that day, the grim bowman had good reason to be so serious.

There's no sense in thinking about nothing *but* problems, or the immensity of them will overwhelm us. Jesus said, "Do not worry about tomorrow, for tomorrow will worry about itself. Each day has enough trouble of its own" (Matthew 6:34 NIV). We *do* need to take today's matters seriously and do want we can to take care of them. Beyond that, however, we simply have to trust God.

51

Messengers Bearing Messages

Suddenly out of the dark something fluttered to his
shoulder. He started—but it was only an old thrush.
Unafraid it perched by his ear and brought him news.
THE HOBBIT, CHAPTER 14

Seeing the bridge gone, Smaug began to circle the town, swooping down repeatedly and setting wooden structures ablaze. Every time he made a pass, the archers loosed a volley of arrows, which, unfortunately, bounced harmlessly off Smaug's impenetrable scales. Soon, despite their best efforts, much of the town was burning.

Citizens and defenders alike leaped into the water, but Bard stood his ground and notched the last arrow to his bow. Just then, a thrush landed on his shoulder and began chattering. Bard was astonished to realize that he *understood* the bird's speech—and *just* as astonished at what it told him.

Talking thrushes? What's *this* all about? Rewind, rewind. . .

Back when Bilbo and the dwarves first discovered the secret door, they noticed a thrush nearby, catching snails. The next day, after Bilbo's talk with Smaug, he told the dwarves he'd seen a soft spot in the hollow of the dragon's left breast. The hobbit noticed the thrush sitting nearby and didn't like the thought of it listening in, but Thorin assured him that these birds were friendly. In fact, the men of Dale could understand them and had once utilized them to take messages to Laketown and back.

And that's precisely what this old thrush did: he set out straightaway for Laketown carrying this vital information to Bard, a man of Dale. Now, armed with this crucial clue, Bard drew back his bow and—as Smaug swooped overhead—sent his last arrow straight through the dragon's soft spot and into its heart. The monster let out a piercing scream, arched back, and then fell headlong into the burning town below. Smaug was dead!

All because an old thrush passed on a very important message.

Now, the idea of talking birds is not as odd as it may seem. Take African Grey Parrots, for example: some of them have been known to speak up to 950 words, and a parakeet named Puck had a vocabulary of 1,728 words. This idea is also found in the Bible: Solomon advised his readers to be careful what they said "because a bird in the sky may carry your words, and a bird on the wing may report what you say" (Ecclesiastes 10:20 NIV).

Tolkien describes *other* birds speaking with the peoples of Middle-earth. Birds carried the news of Smaug's death far and wide. That's how Thranduil's elves found out about the dragon's demise and also how Beorn and the goblins of the Misty Mountains heard the news. The dwarves, for their part, had a rapport with ravens, and as armies began to converge on Lonely Mountain, Thorin sent messages by ravens to his kinsman Dain in the Iron Hills.

Man has always identified birds with winged heavenly beings and angels, and the association is an easy one to make. The very word *angel* means "messenger," which is fitting because this is one of their most important tasks. Angels not only protect us but also bring us messages from God. For example, the angel Gabriel took an important message to the prophet Daniel (Daniel 8:15–17; 9:21–22). Centuries later, this same eternal being told a priest named Zacharias about the coming birth of his son John and also announced the birth of Jesus to His mother, Mary (Luke 1:5–35). Angels also brought messages to Joseph, Mary's betrothed, on three separate occasions (Matthew 1:18–24; 2:13, 19–20).

The one thing angels apparently *don't* do is carry messages from one person to another. For that, we have carrier pigeons—or, if you prefer, e-mails and text messages. We can also use the age-old method of *talking* to others when we need to communicate. That's where problems frequently arise, because human beings do not possess the must-fly-straight-home instincts of carrier pigeons. Instead, we have the all-too-human tendencies to procrastinate, forget, misplace, and garble vital messages.

Imagine if the old thrush had forgotten to pass on the message to Bard or if it had mixed up the details! Everyone in Laketown would've been killed, and Smaug might have gone on to devastate much of Middle-earth.

King Solomon praised the person who is "a trustworthy messenger to the one who sends him" (Proverbs 25:13 NIV), and that's what we should aspire to be—trustworthy messengers. This comes easy for some of us, but *most* of us can (at least from time to time) forget or muddle messages, which sometimes causes major mix-ups.

So what's the solution to these problems? A good start is to pass on important messages without delay, before we become distracted by the 1,001 details of our busy schedule.

Let's be trustworthy messengers.

52

Thranduil's Disaster Relief

*But the king, when he received the prayers of Bard, had pity,
for he was the lord of a good and kindly people.*
THE HOBBIT, CHAPTER 14

Smaug was gone, but before he died, he had set Laketown ablaze and, as he fell dead, smashed its remains
to splinters. Laketown, too, was gone. One in four of its
people had died, and the rest survived by leaping into the
lake or fleeing in boats. And now the survivors grieved the
losses of their families, their community, their homes, and
their belongings.

Winter was arriving, and a cold wind chilled them.
Many were already sick from hypothermia or suffering

from serious burns, and there was little shelter and almost no food. Many people died in the following days, and the survivors suffered hunger. Bard worked tirelessly, organizing care for the sick and injured and overseeing the building of shelters...but the task was overwhelming. So he sent messengers to the elves pleading for help.

The elven king, meanwhile, hearing of Smaug's death and presuming the dwarves dead, had set out for Lonely Mountain to claim their treasure. Bard's messengers met Thranduil's army enroute and begged him to help. The elven king could have just continued on his way, but he was moved with compassion and turned to Laketown. He also gave orders for food and supplies to be sent and trees to be felled and floated downriver to build shelters. Then the elves arrived at Laketown and began helping.

How different was Thorin's reaction! When Bard told the dwarves of the misery of his people and reminded them that Laketown had helped *them* in their time of need, Bilbo thought Thorin would surely respond generously. Instead, the dwarf-king gave a cold refusal. Ebenezer Scrooge had nothing on this guy! Even Roäc the raven advised Thorin to share—but he refused to give them even enough to buy a loaf of bread.[63]

We often hear about earthquakes, tsunamis, floods, fires, droughts, and other disasters—and our TV screens are filled with the suffering these events bring upon thousands and sometimes millions of people. When these kinds of calamities strike, we wonder why God allows them to happen. Then we start to discuss and debate whether He has a direct hand in every catastrophe, or whether they're the result of natural forces set in motion long ago. But honestly, it doesn't help victims of natural disasters much when we sit around and speculate *why* a disaster occurred.

Whatever other purpose God may have for natural disasters, He uses them as opportunities for believers to demonstrate compassion to hurting people.

In New Testament times, when the Christians in Antioch learned that a great famine was coming, they didn't just sit around theorizing *why* it was about to happen; instead, they immediately collected and sent relief money: "So the believers in Antioch decided to send relief to the brothers and sisters in Judea, everyone giving as much as they could" (Acts 11:29 NLT).

There are two things worth noting here: first of all, *everyone* gave, and, secondly, they gave as much as they reasonably *could*. They didn't give *so* much that they themselves were left without the means to pay their bills.

Some of the Christians in Antioch were themselves poor and weren't able to give much at all, but they did something people in all economic classes can do, even today: *pray* for the sufferers. Scripture is clear that we should pray for those in a bad way: "Arise, cry out in the night. . .pour out your heart like water in the presence of the Lord. Lift up your hands to him for the lives of your children, who faint from hunger at every street corner" (Lamentations 2:19 NIV). This doesn't mean a one-time prayer; we are to continue to remember them in prayer as if we ourselves were the ones suffering (Hebrews 13:3).

Many people ask, "What good does prayer do when people are destitute? Money is what's needed." Other people, however, insist that it's equally useless to send money. "What good does that do?" they ask. "It all ends up in the pockets of the relief agencies." And so, like Thorin, they do nothing.

Whether we choose to give financially to those in need, or whether we spend our time and energy in earnest prayer for the hurting, the bottom line is we all can and should do something.

All theoretical musings about why God allows disasters should become irrelevant when we come face-to-face with the genuine needs, even in our own church or community. The apostle John challenged his readers, "If someone has enough money to live well and sees a brother or sister in need but shows no compassion—how can God's love be in that person?" (1 John 3:17 NLT). That's a candid question each of us should ask ourselves from time to time.

Like the dwarves arriving destitute in Laketown, many of us have been the recipients of the kindness of others, so we know what it's like to be in need. Let's make sure we show that same kind of kindness to those we know who are in need.

53
Catching the Dragon-Sickness

But also he did not reckon with the power that gold has upon
which a dragon has long brooded, nor with dwarvish hearts.
THE HOBBIT, CHAPTER 15

When Bard presented his petition to the dwarf-king, he was standing in front of the gate of Erebor with the army of Laketown behind him. With them was the army of the elves. As Thorin stated, if they'd merely come to ask him to donate to a needy cause, why had they assembled two armies? They didn't exactly resemble bell-ringers with donation kettles standing outside a supermarket. The answer was that they, like him, had caught "the dragon-sickness."[64] By this Tolkien meant an inordinate love for gold and wealth.

Smaug, being a dragon, was naturally thoroughly infected. Thorin described him as an especially greedy dragon.[65] But, of course, he *would* say that, for Smaug had stolen all his treasure. When the dwarves saw all their long-lost gold and treasure in the great hall inside the mountain, they, too, fell under "the bewitchment of the hoard."[66] And while you wouldn't normally think of elves as greedy, some of them were. Thranduil was: "If the elf-king had a weakness it was for treasure."[67] Yes, that *would* be considered a weakness!

The Master of Laketown was a materialistic business-man. Bard later gave him a generous share of the treasure to help the destitute people of Laketown, but the Master, overcome with greed, absconded with most of it. (He was a perfect example of the kind of relief organization you should *not* give your hard-earned cash to.) Bard, despite his noble nature, was moved with thoughts of how the treasure of the dwarves would help him rebuild his hometown of Dale—complete with bells of pure gold.

Bilbo fell under the enchantment of the Arkenstone and claimed it for his own, even though he knew full well that it was the most valued heirloom of Thorin's kingdom.

And *orcs*? Don't even get me started. . . .

It seems as if *everyone* was catching dragon-sickness,

though some had it worse than others. Most of them weren't yet rich when gold fever hit them. They became sick just *thinking* about coming into money. Everybody desired to be rich—just like so many of us in real life.

Small wonder that the apostle Paul warned, "Those who desire to be rich fall into temptation and a snare, and into many foolish and harmful lusts which drown men in destruction and perdition. For the love of money is a root of all kinds of evil, for which some have strayed from the faith in their greediness, and pierced themselves through with many sorrows" (1 Timothy 6:9–10 NKJV).

Let's be clear: It's not a sin to *have* money, contrary to what some people think. It is a sin, however, to *love* money. It's not even a sin to *desire* to be rich. After all, many believers are motivated to work hard and earn money so they can turn around and give to needy causes, support orphanages, and fund Christian missions. Many wealthy Christians have been outstanding philanthropists.

Many of us have promised God that we'd do the same things if He blessed us with money. But God often sees fit to spare us the temptations and foolish and harmful lusts that so often accompany wealth.

Paul goes on to give the cure for dragon-sickness: "Command those who are rich in this present world not to be arrogant nor to put their hope in wealth, which is so uncertain, but to put their hope in God. . . . Command them to do good, to be rich in good deeds, and to be generous and willing to share" (1 Timothy 6:17–18 NIV).

The biblical cure is a simple three-step program, and each step leads into the next in a natural progression. The first step is to not put your trust in wealth, meaning don't lust for the stuff (and scramble after it) if you *lack* it and don't lust for it (and greedily clutch it) if you *have* it. The second step is to choose to be rich in good deeds rather than in cold gold. The third and final step is to purpose to do good deeds by sharing financially with those in dire need. (Who'd have seen *that* one coming?)

So where does this leave most of us? Does this mean we're being covetous if we invest in a good education so we can end up with a well-paying career? Are we greedy if we have enough foresight to put aside some retirement savings? No. God knows we have to be able to provide for ourselves and for our families; in fact, He tells us we're not walking in the truth if we don't (1 Timothy 5:8; 2 Thessalonians 3:10).

The question we need to ask ourselves is this: do we trust in our money, or do we trust in God? One way we can determine our own answers to that question is to honestly appraise how tightly we hang on to our surplus cash. . .and how willing we are to share with those in need. This is a very accurate thermometer of just how hot our gold fever burns.

The good news is, even if we have a *touch* of dragon-sickness, we can recover from it.

54

A Misunderstood Friend

"Get down now to your friends!" he said to Bilbo,
"or I will throw you down."
THE HOBBIT, CHAPTER 17

Bilbo and the dwarves were trapped inside Erebor because the front gate was blocked by armies of elves and men. The besiegers couldn't enter because the dwarves had built a wall of stones in front of the gate—and had created a deep lake in front of that. Winter had arrived, and no one had much food. Things had become desperate, but neither side was budging.

One night, Bilbo put on his invisible ring and crept out to the besiegers' camp. He handed Bard the Arkenstone, saying it would aid him in bargaining then sneaked back to the dwarves. The next day, when Bard offered to exchange the Arkenstone for gold, Thorin angrily asked how he had ended up with it. When Bilbo confessed, the dwarf-king nearly hurled him to the rocks below. Only Gandalf's timely appearance saved his life. Then Bilbo told Thorin to exchange *his* (Bilbo's) share of treasure for the gem. The dwarf-king grimly agreed and bitterly announced, "I am betrayed,"[68] then ordered Bilbo out of his sight.

From Thorin's perspective, he *had* been betrayed. He'd always been fair, even generous, to the hobbit. Now, after months of friendship, Mr. Baggins had stabbed him in the back, and he was spitting mad. Although they didn't dare speak up, not all the dwarves agreed with that view. Bombur, Fili, and Kili thought Thorin had been unreasonable to not share his gold. They may not have agreed with *how* Bilbo went about it, but they admired him for giving up his share of the treasure to make peace. As Bilbo departed, several dwarves felt ashamed at the way he was being treated.

Have you ever been in Thorin's dwarf boots? Have you felt undermined by a close friend who disagreed with the way you'd handled a situation or felt you had acted unreasonably? Even if you can admit that you may have been *partially* wrong, do you feel that it justified their lack of loyalty? Should they have stood by you anyway? Once you've had a chance to cool down, it might help to talk to a dwarf who has a second opinion. Or you might want to have a long heart-to-heart chat with Roäc the raven.

Or have you, like Bilbo, *caused* someone to believe you'd betrayed them? Have you clumsily attempted to bring about a fair solution when someone close to you was clearly in the wrong but ended up turning a friend into an enemy? Do you still completely justify your actions, or are you able now to see how it might have looked from the *other* person's perspective?

Or, like Fili and Kili, have you ever stood on the sidelines while two friends, neither of whom were fully right or fully wrong, fought it out? When someone feels betrayed, motives often seem murky and issues not entirely clear.

Abner was captain of King Saul's army. After Saul died, Abner supported Saul's son Ishbosheth as the new king. However, the people of Judah followed David, because God had promised to make *him* king in place of Saul. Abner was aware of the prophecies, but he had remained loyal to Ishbosheth. Since Saul was dead, his concubine, Rizpah, was a free woman, so Abner took her. Normally, someone who married a former king's wife/concubine was in effect declaring *his* claim to the throne. Abner had no such intentions, but that's what Ishbosheth accused him of. This made Abner so upset that he decided to do something that he should've done long ago—hand the kingdom over to David. Yes, the throne "belonged" to Saul's son, but David had a greater claim to it.

As you can imagine, when Abner tried to do the "right" thing (but with such murky motives), he made a complete mess of things. Not only did Ishbosheth feel betrayed, but both he and Abner ended up dead (2 Samuel 3–4).

Situations don't usually end up *that* deadly in real life, but they can lead to a lot of hurt feelings and bitterness. Unfortunately, as Solomon wrote, "An offended friend is harder to win back than a fortified city. Arguments separate friends like a gate locked with bars" (Proverbs 18:19 NLT).

Misunderstandings and arguments *can* be resolved, however. Love can prevail over bitterness, but it takes humility, apologies, and prayer for that to happen.

It happened in Tolkien's tale: as Thorin lay dying after the battle, he took back his angry words and reconciled with Bilbo. That can happen in real life, too—though we can hope it's without the dying part.

There are few things as painful as losing a close friend . . .and few things as wonderful as restoring a friendship. The problem, however, is that pride often prevents us from taking the first step—much as we long to. Ask Jesus to change both your heart and the heart of the friend you've lost due to some disagreement or misunderstanding. He can do miracles, after all.

55

Tearing Down Walls

The dwarf-lord now joined them: the Goblins were the foes of all, and at their coming all other quarrels were forgotten.
THE HOBBIT, CHAPTER 17

Bard's and Thranduil's armies were laying siege to the front gate of Lonely Mountain when, early in the morning, Thorin's cousin Dain arrived from the Iron Hills with five hundred heavily armed dwarves. They were just about to battle the besiegers when—surprise, surprise!—a vast army of goblins arrived. These orcs had assembled in Gundabad to overrun the north of Middle-earth, but they had rushed here first to claim the treasure. With them came an immense host of wargs and monstrous vampire bats.

As the orcs and their axis of evil arrived, Dain's dwarves joined forces with elves and men. This was no small concession! There were deep, historical grievances between elves and dwarves, and recent events had only increased the animosity. For their part, the men of Laketown blamed the dwarves for sending the dragon upon them and causing their misery. But orcs were unimaginably vile and cruel. They had a long history of enslaving, torturing, and killing the Free Peoples of Middle-earth—and their armies were so enormous that unless the quarreling factions immediately united, they'd all be massacred.

And so the Battle of Five Armies began.

However, not *all* the dwarves joined right away. The battle raged for *several hours* before Thorin and company finally realized that they couldn't allow others to fight and die while they hid safely behind their stone wall. Their hatred for orcs and their sense of honor were more important to them than all their gold—or even their very lives. So they knocked down the wall and came charging out into the fray.

About *time*, guys!

But just the same, talk about unlikely allies.

This kind of odd alliance happened in the Bible as well. About four thousand years ago, a great eastern king named Tidal gathered his raiding forces and, leading the combined armies of three other kings, swept like a. . .*well*, tidal wave over the rich cities of east Canaan. Among the people they took captive and carried away was Lot, Abraham's nephew.

Now, Abraham had only 318 men of war—who couldn't *hope* to defeat Tidal's eastern armies—but he was allied with three Amorite leaders. (If you know anything about Amorites, you're probably already questioning Abraham's judgment.) At any rate, Abraham joined forces with the Amorites, attacked Tidal and the eastern kings, and defeated them. He recovered all the captives and wealth they'd taken (Genesis 14).

Now, Amorites worshiped one high god—*plus* seventy-some lesser gods—but they had many beliefs and customs that separated them from the Hebrews. Centuries later, their descendents would become so evil that they were practically synonymous with Canaanites. But at this point in their history they were just. . .well. . .*slightly* bad (Genesis 15:16). Abraham's men probably looked at the Amorites the same way as elves looked at dwarves—never fully trusting them but at least glad they were on their side.

The apostle Paul cautioned against forming close unions with unbelievers, calling it being "unequally yoked together" (2 Corinthians 6:14 KJV). This is a word picture of an ox and a donkey being linked, or yoked, together by a wooden crossbeam and harness, something people of his time knew wouldn't work very well, if at all, because the two animals moved at different speeds.

Paul was referring to *very* close relationships, such as marriages. However, we can't very well avoid working together, day after day, with some people who are far from being Christian. So what are we to do? Insist that everyone working on the assembly line convert? Refuse to be part of a committee unless everyone is a believer? That wouldn't be practical—or even possible. As Paul bluntly told the Christians of Corinth, if they didn't like keeping company with unbelievers, they'd better be prepared to leave this world (1 Corinthians 5:9–10).

Nevertheless, our very *closest* unions and friendships should be with other Christians.

But let's be honest: *Our* problem is that we often have trouble getting along with Christians—the very people we're supposed to get along with *best*. This problem is nothing new in the church. The Christians in Corinth were fractured into a number of exclusive congregations, each one following its own favorite teacher. This, of course, led to doctrinal arguments, jealousy, and quarrels between the factions (1 Corinthians 1:10–13; 3:3–7).

Now, there's nothing wrong with loving to attend a certain fellowship group and feeling a greater sense of belonging there than anywhere else. We all need a home church. It's also understandable that we lean toward one doctrinal teaching more than another. The problem comes, however, when we allow our denominational allegiances to become so strong that they create walls between us and other believers. When church affiliations become barriers and differences become quarrels, it's time to start knocking *down* the walls—like Thorin did.

We don't need to pretend there are no differences between us and other believers—but we do need to *love* them as our brothers and sisters in Christ.

56

A Time for Wild Bears

In that last hour Beorn himself had appeared. . . .
He came alone, and in bear's shape; and he seemed
to have grown almost to giant-size in his wrath.
THE HOBBIT, CHAPTER 18

All day long, the battle raged at the foot of Lonely Mountain. The armies of elves, men, and dwarves fought fiercely but were vastly outnumbered. And as a blood-red sunset drew on, they were about to be overrun. Then the Eagles arrived. They dove down and swept goblins off the mountain ridges like so many tenpins.

Eagles excelled at precision strikes—such as plucking dwarves from fir trees—but they didn't dare land because doing so would make them easy targets. But gigantic monster bears? They're another matter entirely! They're *made* for wading into battlegrounds and mauling orcs. And that's exactly what Beorn did. Just as the day was dying, Beorn arrived in enormous black bear mode and scattered the goblins right and left with his powerful paws. He ripped through the bodyguards and slew the goblin-king, Bolg. Even with the eagles' help, the defenders were *still* being overrun, but once Beorn killed the king, the orcs fled in fear.

While we shouldn't downplay what the Eagles did, Beorn's help was *the* decisive factor in the final hour of the battle. And it breathed new hope and life into the tired defenders.

Beorn was literally superhuman, but there *have* been outstanding real-life heroes in millennia past. Some belonged to an elite cadre called "David's Mighty Men." One of them was a warrior named Adino, who, armed with only a sword, single-handedly killed eight hundred enemy soldiers at one time. Then there was Eleazar, who was about to engage the Philistines in battle when his own men fled in fear. Alone, he attacked an entire army, felling Philistines left and right until his hand was weary. When his men finally returned, Eleazar was the only one standing (2 Samuel 23:8–10). And who can forget strongman Samson, who obliterated an army of one thousand Philistines with a donkey's jawbone (Judges 15:14–15)?

But the *big* question with Beorn is this: Since he was so powerful and his help so badly needed, why did he wait until "the last hour" before showing up? The battle might have ended a lot sooner had he not waited till sundown to arrive. Well, why *was* he late? Because he had so far to travel *and* he was on foot. He couldn't simply fly at high speed like a giant Eagle. Even had he taken the shortest route possible—straight through Mirkwood—he would have traveled nearly 250 miles. Beorn had probably set out the instant he knew his friends were in danger.

When we're hard-pressed and almost overcome by adversity, we may find it easy to wonder why God sometimes waits until the eleventh hour to help us—or to send us help. And then He does a miracle and saves the day. Then, like King David, we say, "If the LORD had not been on our side. . .the flood would have engulfed us, the torrent would have swept over us" (Psalm 124:1, 4 NIV).

But let's be honest. While we're thankful—at least *relieved*—that God finally rescued us, we still ask Him, "Why did You wait so *long*? Why did You allow us to suffer so much first?"

Think of your reaction when a friend promises he'll be there to help you on moving day but only shows up at the *end* to rescue your tired friends who have been carrying heavy furniture up stairs all day. While you're thankful he showed up at all, your question is, "Where *were* you all day?" If he'd been a total stranger who showed up unexpectedly to help. . .hey, no questions asked. But it's different when he's a trusted friend. . .and when he promised.

God is the Friend who promises to be there. He has made many promises in His Word to help us during times of distress and to save us. He *does* save us, yes, and sometimes He does a miracle early on and ends the battle before it even starts. No fuss, no muss. We endure no moving-day stress and no financial worries. Ah! If life were *always* that simple! But it's not. Many times, we have to go *through* the battle. We have to endure much and hang on while we wait for God to work things out.

Tolkien tells us that no one really knew how or from where Beorn had come—which *also* means no one knew why he hadn't arrived sooner. Presumably, he explained everything to their satisfaction after the battle. And so it is with God: We can't always understand why He delays in helping us, but one day we'll have a long heart-to-heart talk with Him. Then we'll understand.

In the meantime, we can be thankful that He *did* a miracle, thankful that, in the end, the flood did *not* sweep over us and the torrent did not engulf us.

57

Simple Pleasures and Priorities

"If more of us valued food and cheer and song above hoarded gold, it would be a merrier world."
THE HOBBIT, CHAPTER 18

Bilbo was wearing his ring during the last hours of the battle. This was wise, since being invisible saved him from being targeted by orcs. Nevertheless, he was still stunned by a chance rock and lay unconscious all night. When he came to the next day and removed his ring, a man saw him and carried him to the camp. Gandalf then took him inside the tent where Thorin lay dying. Thorin was glad to see the hobbit, and he took back the harsh words he had spoken before and then made his famous statement above.

Then he died—a tragic but repentant figure.

Thorin had hoarded his treasure, but as his life was slipping away, his sense of priorities came into sharp focus.

The Bible repeatedly urges us to keep material possessions in proper perspective, simply because we can't take them with us when we leave this life. As the apostle Paul wrote, "For we brought nothing into this world, and it is certain we can carry nothing out" (1 Timothy 6:7 KJV). Or as Thorin said, it was time for him to leave his gold and silver and go to the Halls of Waiting, where his vast treasure would be of little value.

Note that Thorin said it was better to value food and cheer and song above *hoarded* gold. Gold, in itself, if shared generously, can be a very good thing. After all, it takes a certain amount of gold to pay for a cheery feast. Thorin hadn't been wrong to attempt to recover the gold that rightfully belonged to him, either. His fault had been in *hoarding* it and in refusing to share it with the people of Laketown. They were starving, despairing, and in need of cheer—and even a modest donation on Thorin's part would have helped provide that food and cheer.

These words of Jesus are particularly pertinent to this situation: "Take heed and beware of covetousness, for one's life does not consist in the abundance of the things he possesses" (Luke 12:15 NKJV).

Jesus then told a parable about a rich man whose fields had yielded bumper crops—so much so that his existing granaries couldn't contain his overflowing harvest. He could have shared his surplus freely with the poor or sold it to them at a compassionate rate, but instead he decided to build greater barns, hoard every bit of his wealth, and retire in luxury. His advice to himself was, "Soul, you have many goods laid up for many years; take your ease; eat, drink, and be merry." But God told him he was going to die that very night, so he wouldn't benefit one iota from his hoarded riches. Jesus summed up this lesson: "So is he who lays up treasure for himself, and is not rich toward God" (Luke 12:19–21 NKJV).

How do we become "rich toward God?" By doing good and sharing with others. The rich fool in Jesus' parable had the same problem as Thorin. It wasn't wrong for him to want to "eat, drink, and be merry," but he wanted it all, and that *was* wrong. He turned his eyes away from those around him who were desperate and needed "food and cheer and song" even more than he did.

In the end, that is what Thorin came to appreciate about hobbits—and what Gandalf had loved most about Shire-folk for two centuries already. During the terrible Long Winter, 182 years earlier, the hobbits were dying from the bitter cold and starving in the famine that followed.

Gandalf was deeply moved to see them in such a terrible crisis but still having pity on one another and sharing what very little they had. Hobbits had a strong sense of compassion and community, and it was these qualities that had helped them survive as a people.[69]

Even when we're struggling to make ends meet, we can still enjoy some of the greatest riches this world has to offer. We build strong, happy bonds that last a lifetime when we take time out of our busy schedules to come together for a gathering of family or friends. Moments like those are worth far more than money. The food may be good for our bodies, but the cheer is even better for our souls.

As King Solomon, the wealthiest man who ever lived, observed, *true* wealth has to do with attitude. Whether rich or poor, "he who is of a merry heart has a continual feast" (Proverbs 15:15 NKJV). Here's another of Solomon's sayings: "A feast is made for laughter" (Ecclesiastes 10:19 KJV). The point of getting together with loved ones is to eat, drink, and be merry. . .*together*.

And when someone we hadn't planned on feeding shows up. . .well, the more the merrier!

58

Faraway, Enchanting Lands

*It was spring. . .before Bilbo and Gandalf took
their leave at last of Beorn, and though he
longed for home, Bilbo left with regret.*
THE HOBBIT, CHAPTER 18

Throughout his adventure—especially during difficult, dreary, or dangerous days—Bilbo wished he were back in his own home, sleeping in his own downy feather bed or puttering about in his beloved kitchen. Now that the Battle of Five Armies was over, the dragon dead, and Dain established as King under the Mountain, Mr. Baggins ached to return home. So he and Gandalf set out, accompanied by Beorn. At first, the hobbit refused to take any treasure, but Dain talked him into taking a small chest each of gold and silver.

Winter had already begun, and snow would soon be swirling down, making traveling cold and the road difficult, so when they arrived back at Beorn's home by midwinter, they had little choice but to settle in and hunker down. They couldn't cross the Misty Mountains in this winter weather, and where else could they stay? So Bilbo was forced to shift out of his *I-wanna-go-home* mode.

They stayed with Beorn about three full months. You can imagine the *long* conversations they had! And men from all over Wilderland joined them—for Beorn had broken off his sullen solitude and invited them. The Battle of Five Armies apparently helped him work through his anger issues, because his Yule celebrations were downright merry! Spring finally burst forth around Beorn's longhouse, and blossoms were everywhere. Mr. Baggins loved flowers, and after being snowed in for months, he was so overcome by the beauty that he scarcely wanted to leave.

But he *did* leave. He still longed to go home, after all.

After lengthy absences, we, too, sometimes just want to head back to well-known surroundings and familiar faces. Exploring new vistas certainly enlarges our horizons, challenges us, and—unless we're total sticks-in-the-mud—is invigorating as well. For example, while some of us are homebodies, most of us were eager to launch out from our parents' home when we came of age. This is especially true for those of us who viewed life at home as...well...*less* than perfect. Even then, passing years usually mellow negative memories, so there's always a side that longs to return to childhood haunts, to talk to old friends, and to walk familiar paths.

Perhaps we've simply moved to another city for work or for education, so we had to leave familiar surroundings and loved ones behind. Then, when the opportunity to return arises, we eagerly anticipate it. But we often find that although home still has an allure, it's not the same. And *we're* not the same once we've seen the wider world, either. We now appreciate other things and have a larger vision. We're forever changed. That's why, years later, Bilbo had had *enough* of the Shire and the familiar faces and longed to get out and see mountains again. So he packed up and moved to Rivendell.[70]

There will be times in life when you feel very deeply rooted. There will be other times—perhaps many of them—when you'll feel uprooted and displaced, as if you don't really belong *anywhere*. Or you may feel that you belong to both places at once.

Those who emigrated from another country understand these mixed emotions well. While they may still identify their former country as their homeland, the place of their roots, they find that, as the years go by, their new nation has more of a feeling of *home*. They may still enjoy visiting their old country—with an emphasis on *visiting*—but they still wish to return to their new, adopted country. It's now their country, after all.

It may seem odd to think of someone feeling like a mere visitor in their country, but it's a common feeling. The Bible talks about these kinds of feelings. It says of those who follow God, "They agreed that they were foreigners and nomads here on earth. Obviously people who say such things are looking forward to a country they can call their own. If they had longed for the country they came from, they could have gone back. But they were looking for a better place, a heavenly homeland. That is why God is not ashamed to be called their God, for he has prepared a city for them" (Hebrews 11:13–16 NLT).

As Christians, we've gone through deep changes and have a new sense of values, and this often distances us from some family members and old friends. We find ourselves no longer fitting into our former culture. We've become like "foreigners and exiles" (1 Peter 2:11 NIV). We're still living in this world, but we feel almost like we don't *quite* belong here anymore. And in a very real way, we don't, for heaven is our true homeland.

Once a faraway land of enchanting beauty has captured our imaginations, we are never the same.

59

A Heavenly Haven

Then the elves of the valley came out and greeted them
and led them across the water to the house of Elrond.
THE HOBBIT, CHAPTER 19

Thorin and company had stopped in Rivendell in June of the previous year, and now, on May 1, eleven months later, Bilbo and Gandalf finally arrived back at the elvish haven. The elves were overjoyed at their arrival, and as soon as hobbit and wizard descended into the wooded valley, they came out to greet them and led them across the River Bruinen into the refuge of Rivendell, where the two road-weary travelers rested for a week before continuing on their journey.

Elves loved beautiful things—poetry and song and dancing, nature and gardens and trees—and they were highly skilled in making things of transcendent beauty. Thus Rivendell, although it was not large, was a gem of elvish architecture and landscaping. And since Elrond wore Vilya, one of the three elvish Rings of Power, Rivendell was a protected sanctuary. Tolkien tells us, "Evil things did not come into that valley."[71]

At one time, elves had lived in great numbers throughout Middle-earth, but over the long centuries, they had obeyed the summons of the Valar to depart mortal lands, cross the sea by the "straight road," and come to Valinor, the Undying Lands in the West. Only a few High Elves still lingered in Middle-earth, and (apart from Thranduil's Wood-elves in Mirkwood) they chiefly resided in three realms—Rivendell under Elrond, Lórien under Galadriel, and the Grey Havens (Mithlond) under Círdan. Because both Elrond and Galadriel wore an elvish Ring of Power, which enhanced their natural powers, they were able, so to speak, to create a little piece of heaven on Middle-earth.

Elrond and Galadriel created and sustained their beautiful sanctuaries for long ages, but they left even them behind when they set sail for the Undying Lands.

We, too, must one day obey God's summons and step into eternity. As Christians, we can be certain we have eternal life and can take comfort in knowing that heaven is our eternal home. The apostle John describes how, after a lifetime of tribulation and toil, God's children are comforted in heaven: "Therefore they are before the throne of God, and serve Him day and night in His temple. And He who sits on the throne will dwell among them. They shall neither hunger anymore nor thirst anymore; the sun shall not strike them, nor any heat; for the Lamb who is in the midst of the throne will shepherd them and lead them to living fountains of waters. And God will wipe away every tear from their eyes" (Revelation 7:15–17 NKJV).

This is wonderful news, but in the meantime, while we're still on earth, we long to find peace and rest from our daily trials and pressing concerns. Like the elves, we need a sanctuary here and now. Far too many of us, however, seek to fulfill this legitimate need for a little heaven on Earth with material things. Instead of waiting until we arrive in heaven to get a mansion, we try to acquire one in this life. We seek to create a beautiful sanctuary complete with fish ponds and gardens and fountains, sunken living rooms, exquisite paintings, and high-end décor. We reward ourselves with every comfort and luxury our hearts long for.

And often we *still* don't find true and lasting peace and satisfaction. Even in the midst of such tranquility and beauty, we're burdened down and our spirits aren't refreshed. Why?

The reason is simple: Although a beautiful garden or home can inspire us on *one* level, what truly makes heaven paradise is being in the presence of God. It's the Lord who refreshes us, comforts us, and wipes away tears from our eyes—not only in the future but even now. We just have to enter His sanctuary, into His presence: "He who dwells in the secret place of the Most High shall abide under the shadow of the Almighty. I will say of the LORD, 'He is my refuge and my fortress; my God, in Him I will trust'" (Psalm 91:1–2 NKJV).

While personal quiet time with God is a must, He also intends that we enter His sanctuary in the company of other believers. Jesus promised, "For where two or three are gathered together in my name, there am I in the midst of them" (Matthew 18:20 KJV). And when Jesus is present, He soothes our troubled minds and breathes strength into our spirits. There's joy in community. Remember, in heaven we'll all be worshiping God together.

We will only truly know full joy when we get to heaven, but we *can* enjoy a measure of God's presence *this* side of paradise as well—both within our personal quiet place and with other believers.

60

Your Place in God's Plans

"You don't really suppose, do you, that all your adventures and
escapes were managed by mere luck, just for your sole benefit?"
THE HOBBIT, CHAPTER 19

A little over a month after leaving Rivendell, Bilbo
once again walked through the Shire, the land he
loved and knew so well. He eagerly anticipated seeing his
beloved hobbit hole again. But to his amazement, he discovered that because of his lengthy absence, he'd been pre-
sumed dead. He arrived home in the last throes of a public
auction in which all his earthly possessions had already
been sold. Worse yet, many of his neighbors refused to accept the fact that he was *actually* Bilbo Baggins returned,

so in the end, he was forced to buy back most of his own belongings.

And then he settled back into his comfortable hobbit hole. *Sigh*...

Seven years later, Bilbo's friends Gandalf and Balin showed up at his door. They told him the news from the north, and Bilbo was happy to learn that prosperity had returned to Laketown. New songs were being sung, in fact, celebrating the fact that the rivers were now running with gold. When Bilbo expressed surprise that the prophecies had actually come true, Gandalf asked why it amazed him. Was it because he'd *helped* bring them about and couldn't believe he'd been part of something so big? Or was he so focused on himself that he still hadn't seen the larger picture?

The truth was, as Gandalf pointed out, there had been far more than some personal "good luck" at work repeatedly saving Bilbo from danger and imprisonment—as if he were the only one who really mattered. There was far more at stake than just him; there was a larger power at work with a larger plan in mind. That power was Eru Ilúvatar, who guided the destinies of *all* the peoples of Middle-earth.

And so it is in real life: God is intensely interested in each one of us personally, and He manages the details so that His plan for our individual lives works out. But at the same time, He has the Big Picture in mind. God is just as concerned about others as well, and whatever He does in our lives isn't for *our* benefit only.

None of us is an end in ourselves. We are social beings who dwell in communities, and one of the most persistent commandments in the Bible—particularity in the New Testament—is that we love our fellow man. God is deeply concerned that we care about others and do good *to* them and *for* them.

Yes, it's vitally important that we believe that God loves us personally. Jesus died on the cross to bring *us* back into relationship with His Father. Once we've accepted Christ as our Savior, God's Spirit dwells in our hearts, giving each of us a personal relationship with Him. We should be deeply comforted in knowing that He knows each one of us by name, that He listens to our prayers, and, above all, that He *loves* us.

But our personal relationship with God cannot be an all-consuming end in itself. While it *is* important to know that God loves us and that He wants us to love Him in return, the Bible tells us that love for others is a natural outgrowth of that love relationship:

Beloved, let us love one another, for love is of God; and everyone who loves is born of God and knows God. He who does not love does not know God, for God is

love. . . . Beloved, if God so loved us, we also ought to love one another. . . . If someone says, "I love God," and hates his brother, he is a liar; for he who does not love his brother whom he has seen, how can he love God whom he has not seen? And this commandment we have from Him: that he who loves God must love his brother also.
1 JOHN 4:7–8, 11, 20–21 NKJV

Often, like Bilbo, we can become so focused on our own personal fortunes (or *mis*fortunes) that they're pretty much all that concerns us. Likewise, we can become so wrapped up in our own relationship with God that we fail to understand how we fit into His plans for others. We come to believe that we're so special that, for all intents and purposes, we *are* God's plan. Since God loves us so much, and since we're His beloved children, we can sometimes think nothing is too good for us. In short, our outlook can become downright self-centered.

While God wants us to enjoy ourselves and to delight in the ways He blesses us, He knows—and wants us to know—that our greatest joy is found in loving Him then serving Him and others. Only then will we truly live.

That's why we all need a Gandalf to come along every now and again to stir us up, to inspire us to take part in some great adventure, and to remind us that there's a wide, needy world out there beyond our doorstep.

Glossary of Terms

Anduin River—Called the Great River in *The Hobbit*, this river flowed north-south between the Misty Mountains and Mirkwood.

Arkenstone of Thrain—A great, glittering white gem discovered under Lonely Mountain by Thrain the Old, and called the Heart of the Mountain.

Azog—The father of Bolg, this goblin was infamous for killing Thror in Moria.

Back Door—The goblins' lower gate on the eastern slopes of the Misty Mountains.

Balin—The second-oldest dwarf on the quest; he had sharp eyes and was the lookout.

Balrogs—Fallen Maiar that took the form of giant demons, controlling shadow and fire.

Bard—A descendant of Girion, king of Dale; he was leader of the bowmen of Laketown and a counselor to the town's Master.

Battle of Five Armies—The battle at Lonely Mountain where elves, dwarves, and men united to fight goblins and wargs.

Battle of the Mines of Moria—Also called the Battle of Azanulbizar, this was the last great battle in the Dwarf and Goblin War.

Beorn—A powerful man who had the ability to transform himself into a giant black bear.

Bilbo Baggins—The hobbit hero of the story *The Hobbit*.

Blue Hills (also called Blue Mountains)—See *Ered Luin*.

Bolg—The goblin king of Gundabad and son of Azog, who was slain by Beorn.

Carrock—The name Beorn gave to a small, rocky island in the Anduin River.

Celebrimbor—The leader of the elvish smiths; he made the nineteen Rings of Power.

Círdan—Círdan the Shipwright was the ancient elf who ruled Grey Havens.

Dain—The leader of the dwarves of the Iron Hills; he was Thorin's kinsman.

Dale—A town just to the south of Lonely Mountain, famous for its toy market.

Dol Guldur (also called Hill of Sorcery)—Sauron's hilltop fortress in southwest Mirkwood.

Dorwinion—A grape-growing region in the south of the Celduin (River Running).

Durin—The eldest of the Seven Fathers of the Dwarves. He founded the house of Durin, also called the Longbeards or Durin's Folk.

Durin's Day—The dwarves' New Year; the last New Moon before winter, specifically called Durin's Day when the moon and the setting sun were visible together.

Durin's Folk—See *Durin*.

Dwarf and Goblin War (also called the War of the Dwarves and Orcs)—After Azog killed Thror, Thrain summoned all the dwarf clans to war against the goblins of the Misty Mountains. The war ended with a dwarvish victory.

Dwarves—A race of manlike beings, under four feet tall, stocky and very strong; they generally live 250 years.

Eagles—A race of giant, sentient eagles that at times helped the Free Peoples of Middle-earth.

Edge of the Wild—The western edge of Wilderland, beginning at the River Mithiethel.

Elrond—The wise, ancient elf-lord of Rivendell; the father of Arwen.

Enchanted River—A river in north-central Mirkwood, enchanted with elvish magic.

Erebor—The Sindarin name for Lonely Mountain.

Ered Luin (Blue Mountains)—Thorin's people lived in exile there, northwest of the Shire.

Eriador—The lands west of the Misty Mountains; Eriador means "wilderness" in Sindarin.

Eru—Eru Ilúvatar (the Father of All) was the great, good deity the Free Peoples of Middle-earth honored.

Free Peoples (of the World, i.e., of Middle-earth)—Elves, humans, and dwarves—as opposed to nonfree peoples such as goblins.

Frodo—Bilbo's nephew and heir; years later he took the One Ring to Mordor.

Gandalf—The wisest of the five Istari (wizards), he appeared as an old man with a staff; Gandalf means "Elf of the Staff," since many supposed him to be an elf.

Glamdring—The name of Gandalf's elvish sword; Glamdring means "Foe-hammer."

Goblin—An evil race of degraded beings, the villains of Middle-earth, formed by Morgoth from tortured elves; also called orcs.

Gollum—Originally a hobbit named Sméagol, corrupted by the One Ring.

Great Goblin—The unnamed goblin king of the Misty Mountains whom Gandalf slew.

Grey Havens—A port on the west coast of Middle-earth from which elves set sail to Valinor.

Gundabad, Mount—A mountain that rises where the Misty Mountains nearly meet the Grey Mountains from the east.

High Pass—The highest passage over the Misty Mountains east of Rivendell.

Hobbits—A peaceful, agrarian race of humans, averaging three to three and a half feet in height. They lived in the Shire, though some lived in Bree and along the Anduin.

Istari—Wizards; an Order of Maiar the Valar sent from Valinor to Middle-earth to check the resurgent power of Sauron.

Laketown—A trade town on the western shore of Long Lake; also called Esgaroth.

Legolas—The son of Thranduil (he isn't mentioned in *The Hobbit*).

Lonely Mountain—A solitary mountain northeast of Mirkwood, formerly the kingdom of Durin's Folk.

Long Lake—The great lake at the junction of Forest River and River Running.

Lórien—An elvish haven created and maintained by Galadriel. It lay between Moria and Dol Guldur.

Maiar—Lesser angel-like beings who helped the Valar. Gandalf was a Maia. Sauron and the Balrogs were fallen Maiar.

Middle-earth—The main land mass in Arda (Earth), very roughly corresponding to Eurasia and Africa in Earth's distant past.

Mirkwood—Formerly called Greenwood the Great, this vast forest fell under the influence of Sauron and became known as Mirkwood (Dark Forest).

Misty Mountains—The great north-south mountain range east of Eriador and the Shire.

Mithril—Also called Moria-silver or true-silver, it was the most precious metal in Middle-earth, found only in Moria.

Morgoth—Originally called Melkor, he was the most powerful of the Valar. He fell from his lofty position and became the dark lord.

Moria—Khazad-dûm, called Moria ("Black Chasm") in Sindarin, was founded by Durin, and became the richest and most fabulous of the dwarves' cavern-palaces.

Necromancer—One who communicates with the dead (also see *Sauron*).

Old Forest Road—The main east-west road crossing through central Mirkwood.

One Ring—Sauron created a Ring to enslave all who wore the Rings of Power and poured his spirit and malice into it. To Bilbo, it was just a ring that made him invisible.

Orcrist—The name of Thorin's elvish sword; Orcrist means "Orc-cleaver."

Orcs—See *Goblins*.

Radagast—A good wizard, he had a special rapport with birds and beasts.

Rings of Power—The nineteen rings Celebrimbor made that enhanced their bearers' power.

Rivendell—The elvish haven established by Elrond in the valley of the River Bruinen.

Saruman—A formerly good wizard; the head of the Order of Istari.

Sauron—The Maia who served as Morgoth's second-in-command and took his place as dark lord after Morgoth was imprisoned by the Valar.

Shire, The—The English name for Sûza, the hobbits' homeland in central Eriador.

Sindarin—The main language spoken by the elves of Middle-earth.

Smaug—The dragon that attacked Lonely Mountain, killed the dwarves, and hoarded their gold.

Spiders—Giant, evil, sentient spiders that inhabited Mirkwood; lesser descendants of Shelob.

Sting—The name Bilbo gave to the elvish knife he used as a short sword.

Thorin Oakenshield—King of Durin's Folk; he was son of Thrain, son of Thror, and led the dwarves' quest to Lonely Mountain.

Thrain—Thorin's father; he was later captured by the Necromancer (Sauron).

Thrain the Old—Thorin's great-grandfather.

Thranduil—The unnamed elf-king of the Wood-elves of Mirkwood; father of Legolas.

Thror—Thorin's grandfather; his death sparked the Dwarf and Goblin War.

Tooks—An oft-adventuresome clan of hobbits living in the Green Hills of the Shire.

Trolls—Large, powerful, evil, dim-witted beings; the three in *The Hobbit* were William, Tom, and Bert.

Valar—The greatest angel-like beings (Powers) created by Eru; they helped create the world and took care of Middle-earth.

Valinor—The great land across the sea from Middle-earth, home of the Valar and Maiar, and ultimate home of the elves; also called the Undying Lands.

Wargs—Large, evil wolves; they were sentient beings and had their own language.

White Council—Also called the Council of the Wise, it consisted of Gandalf, Saruman, Galadriel, Elrond, Círdan, and other rulers of the elves.

White Wizards—The five Istari: Gandalf, Saruman, Radagast, Alatar, and Pallando.

Wilderland—The wild lands stretching from the River Mithiethel (the Hoarwell) just west of Rivendell all the way to the lands east of Mirkwood.

Wizards—See *Istari* and *Maiar*.

Wood-elves—The Silvan Elves who, in *The Hobbit*, dwelt in the northeast of Mirkwood.

Woodsmen—Men from the south who migrated north to dwell in the western edge of Mirkwood and all along the valley of the River Anduin and its tributaries.

Timeline of *The Hobbit*

Despite the appearance that *The Hobbit* is an entirely spontaneous and unplanned story, Tolkien put considerable thought into the underlying plot. Not only did he repeatedly give the exact number of days it took Thorin and company to travel from one point to another, but also he often noted the phase of the moon, and sometimes the actual day of the week. To work out a realistic chronology, therefore, all these times, lunar phases, and days of the week must line up. Distances, terrain, and travel speed must also be taken into account. Now, the cycles of the moon *repeat* themselves over the millennia, and I've found that the 1995 Lunar Calendar (check it out online) matches perfectly the events of the Quest of Erebor in the year 2941 T.A.

In the timeline below, AH stands for information from *The Annotated Hobbit (Appendix A)*, and UT stands for *Unfinished Tales (The Quest of Erebor)*. The bolded dates are dates that Tolkien himself has given us, and that we know for certain. All other dates are estimates but, I believe, fairly accurate.

2941 T.A.

Mar. 13—Gandalf meets Thorin near Bree in the middle of March (AH).

Mar. 27—They arrive in Ered Luin (after riding 350 miles in 14 days at 25 mi/day).

Mar. 28–30—Gandalf visits Thorin for three days in Ered Luin.

Apr. 5—Bilbo goes walking, hoping to meet elves the next day on their New Year (UT). Gandalf arrives in Hobbiton (after riding 4 days at 50 mi/day), but misses Bilbo.

Apr. 6—The elves' New Year (UT footnote); Gandalf heads back to Thorin.

Apr. 9—Gandalf back in Ered Luin; he tells the dwarves to get ready, then rides off (AH).

Apr. 15—Gandalf is back after one week then rides on ahead to the Shire (AH).

Apr. 25—Dwarves arrive in Bywater (200 mi in 10 days at 20 mi/day).

Apr. 25—Gandalf visits Bilbo that morning (AH).

Apr. 26—Gandalf and the dwarves visit Bilbo (AH).

Apr. 27—Thorin and company leave the inn in Bywater at 11:00 a.m.

May 26—Bilbo notes that it will soon be June; they encounter the trolls at night.

June 6—Thorin and company arrive in Rivendell about eleven days later.

June 20—Midsummer's Eve—the moon is a "broad crescent" (after about fourteen days there).

June 21—Midsummer's Day—Thorin and company leave Rivendell that morning.

July 10—Thorin and company are captured by goblins Monday night.

July 13—Thorin and company flee to the wolves' clearing the next Thursday. They are rescued by the Eagles (on the day after a Full Moon).

July 14—The Eagles carry them to the Carrock the next day.

July 16—Thorin and company leave Beorn's after two days (they travel four days, July 16–19).

July 19—They arrive at Mirkwood on the fourth day.

July 20—Thorin and company enter Mirkwood; Gandalf rides south to the Council.

July 27—They cross the Enchanted River on day seven, halfway through Mirkwood.

Aug. 1—They interrupt the elves' first autumn feasts then are captured by spiders.

Aug. 2—Thorin and company are freed from the spiders then captured by elves.

Aug. 12—Bilbo lives alone in the elf-king's palace (about 10 days).

Aug. 27—Bilbo discovers the twelve dwarves' prisons after a couple weeks (about 14 days).

Sept. 6—Bilbo discovers Thorin's solitary cell (about 10 days later).

Sept. 21—Bilbo and the dwarves escape (about fourteen days later) the night of a great autumn feast.

Sept. 22—Bilbo and the dwarves arrive in Laketown (on Bilbo's birthday). Gandalf is finishing his business and ready to go searching for his friends.

Oct. 6—After a fortnight (two weeks) in Laketown, Thorin announces that they'll leave.

Oct. 9—Thorin and company leave Laketown.

Oct. 10—Thorin and company reach the River Running in two days.

Oct. 11—Thorin and company beach the boats at the end of the third day.

Oct.15—Thorin and company reach Lonely Mountain.

Oct. 20—Bilbo discovers the steps and the secret door.

Oct. 24—(Dark Moon) Thorin says that the last week of autumn begins the next day.

Oct. 25—Durin's Day (last New Moon before winter); Bilbo first enters Smaug's lair.

Oct. 26—Smaug attacks Laketown that night, burns it, but is killed by Bard.

Oct. 29—Thorin and company learn of Smaug's death three days after his demise.

Oct. 31—The elves arrive at the remains of Laketown five days after it has burned.

Nov. 1—The first day of winter.

Nov. 3—Fili and Kili return after four days looking for and finding their pack horses.

Nov. 5—The armies of elves and men set out eleven days after Smaug's death.

Nov. 10—Their united armies arrive at Lonely Mountain after about five days.

Nov. 22—Bilbo sneaks to the enemy ("no moon" = Dark Moon); Dain is two days away.

Nov. 24—Dain and 500 dwarves arrive; the Battle of Five Armies begins.

Nov. 25—Bilbo is taken to see Thorin, who is dying, and who makes amends.

Dec. 21—Bilbo and Gandalf reach Beorn's by midwinter (the winter solstice).

Dec. 21–23—Bilbo and Gandalf are with Beorn during Yule.

Mar. 21—Bilbo and Gandalf leave Beorn's in the spring after about three months.

May 1—Bilbo and Gandalf arrive in Rivendell.

June 22—Bilbo and Gandalf arrive back at Bilbo's home in the Shire.

Sources

Anderson, Douglas A. *The Annotated Hobbit—Revised and Expanded Edition* (Boston/New York: Houghton Mifflin, 2002).

Carpenter, Humphrey, and Christopher Tolkien. *The Letters of J.R.R. Tolkien* (London: George Allen and Unwin, 1981).

Tolkien, J.R.R. *The Hobbit* (London: George Allen and Unwin, 1966).

———. *The Lord of the Rings—The Fellowship of the Ring* (London: George Allen and Unwin, 1954).

———. *The Lord of the Rings—The Return of the King* (London: George Allen and Unwin, 1955).

———. *The Lord of the Rings—The Two Towers* (London: George Allen and Unwin, 1954).

———. *The Tolkien Reader* (New York: Ballantine Books, 1966).

Tolkien, J.R.R., and Christopher Tolkien. *The Silmarillion* (London: George Allen and Unwin, 1977).

———. *Unfinished Tales* (London: George Allen and Unwin, 1980).

Notes

1. *The Letters of J.R.R. Tolkien*, letter 131.
2. *The Fellowship of the Ring*, "Prologue: Concerning Hobbits."
3. *The Hobbit*, chapter 1.
4. *The Fellowship of the Ring*, book 1, chapter 1.
5. *The Hobbit*, chapter 1.
6. *The Return of the King*, appendix A, III, "Durin's Folk."
7. *Unfinished Tales*, "The Quest of Erebor."
8. *The Fellowship of the Ring*, "Prologue: Concerning Hobbits."
9. *The Fellowship of the Ring*, book 2, chapter 4.
10. *Unfinished Tales*, "The Quest of Erebor."
11. *The Hobbit*, chapter 2.
12. *The Hobbit*, chapter 2.
13. *The Hobbit*, chapter 4.
14. *The Fellowship of the Ring*, book 2, chapter 5.
15. *The Hobbit*, chapter 3.
16. *Unfinished Tales*, "The Quest of Erebor."
17. *The Hobbit*, chapter 3.
18. *The Return of the King*, appendix B, "The Tale of Years" (Aragorn was born on March 1, 2931 T.A., and Thorin and company arrived at Rivendell in June 2041).
19. *The Fellowship of the Ring*, book 1, chapter 3.
20. *The Return of the King*, book 6, chapter 9.
21. *The Hobbit*, chapter 4.
22. *The Return of the King*, appendix A, III, "Durin's Folk."
23. *The Hobbit*, chapter 1.
24. *The Letters of J.R.R. Tolkien*, letter 156.
25. *Unfinished Tales*, "The Istari."
26. *The Hobbit*, chapter 5.
27. *The Fellowship of the Ring*, book 1, chapter 2.
28. *The Hobbit*, chapter 5.
29. *The Silmarillion*, "Of the Rings of Power."
30. *The Fellowship of the Ring*, book 1, chapter 2.
31. *The Letters of J.R.R. Tolkien*, letter 156.
32. *The Hobbit*, chapter 10.

33. *The Hobbit*, chapter 6.
34. *The Return of the King*, appendix A, II, "The House of Eorl."
35. *The Hobbit*, chapter 7.
36. Ibid.
37. *The Hobbit*, chapter 18; *The Fellowship of the Ring*, book 2, chapter 1.
38. *The Hobbit*, chapter 6.
39. *The Letters of J.R.R. Tolkien*, letter 156.
40. *Unfinished Tales*, "The Quest of Erebor."
41. *The Return of the King*, appendix B, "The Tale of Years."
42. *The Hobbit*, chapter 7.
43. *The Fellowship of the Ring*, book 2, chapter 6.
44. *The Silmarillion*, "Of the Rings of Power."
45. *The Hobbit*, chapter 9.
46. *The Return of the King*, book 3, chapter 2.
47. *The Tolkien Reader*, "On Fairy Stories."
48. *The Hobbit*, chapter 1.
49. *The Hobbit*, chapter 10.
50. Ibid.
51. *The Fellowship of the Ring*, book 1, chapter 2.
52. *The Hobbit*, chapter 11.
53. *The Annotated Hobbit*, appendix A.
54. *Unfinished Tales*, "The Quest of Erebor."
55. Ibid.
56. *The Hobbit*, chapter 11.
57. *The Hobbit*, chapter 12.
58. *The Annotated Hobbit*, appendix A.
59. *The Fellowship of the Ring*, book 2, chapter 4.
60. Ibid.
61. *The Fellowship of the Ring*, book 2, chapter 5.
62. *The Hobbit*, chapter 1.
63. *The Hobbit*, chapter 15.
64. *The Hobbit*, chapter 19.
65. *The Hobbit*, chapter 1.
66. *The Hobbit*, chapter 13.
67. *The Hobbit*, chapter 8.
68. *The Hobbit*, chapter 17.

69. *Unfinished Tales*, "The Quest of Erebor."
70. *The Fellowship of the Ring*, book 1, chapter 1.
71. *The Hobbit*, chapter 3.